Color on Metal

Color on Metal

50 Artists Share Insights and Techniques

Tim McCreight • **Nicole Bsullak**

GUILD Publishing, Madison, Wisconsin

Distributed by North Light Books, Cincinnati, Ohio

Color on Metal
50 Artists Share Insights and Techniques

Tim McCreight
Nicole Bsullak

Copyright © 2001 by GUILD Publishing

Design: Jane Tenenbaum
Chief Editorial Officer: Katie Kazan
Editor: Dawn Barker
Editorial Assistant: Nikki Muenchow
Photography / pages 8–14: Robert Diamante

01 02 03 04 05 06 07 7 6 5 4 3 2 1

Published by
GUILD Publishing
An imprint of GUILD.com
931 East Main Street
Madison, WI 53703 USA
TEL 608-227-4144 • TEL 877-284-8453 • FAX 608-227-4179

Distributed to the trade and art markets in North America by
North Light Books
An imprint of F&W Publications, Inc.
1507 Dana Avenue
Cincinnati, OH 45207
TEL 800-289-0963

Printed in China

ISBN 1-893164-06-3

Front cover artwork: Helen Shirk, *Commemorative Cup I*, copper, patina and Prismacolor, 18" x 11" x 5". From the collection of the Mint Museum of Craft + Design, Charlotte, North Carolina. Museum purchase: a gift in honor of Bruce and Margo Evans. Photo by David Ramsey. This piece is also shown on the title page.

Back cover artwork: Mary Kanda, mixed long- and short-leaf brooches, glass beads, silver, torch-fired glass and tile grout, 1" x 4$\frac{1}{4}$" and 1$\frac{1}{2}$" x 2$\frac{1}{2}$". Photo by Dean Powell.

**GUILD Publishing is an imprint of GUILD.com, which sells works of art on the Internet.
Visit us, day or night, at www.guild.com.**

CONTENTS

ACKNOWLEDGMENTS

We would like to thank the hundreds of talented artists who allowed us to review their work for this book. If size really didn't matter, we would have included all of them. Special thanks to the 50 artists whose work you'll find here. Their professionalism, support and enthusiasm have made this project a pleasure. Finally, thanks to Jenny Hall for her help in managing the data, Dempsey for his boost to morale, and Scott Miller for support.

Nik Bsullak and Tim McCreight

INTRODUCTION

The history of coloration on metal coincides with the history of metal refining. To a modern mind, the word *metal* conjures a shiny piece of silvery, golden or yellow material. To our ancestors, what metal they saw as raw

An example of natural color on metal: the roof of a farmhouse in England.
Photo by Tim McCreight.

material was as often as not adorned with an organic skin. This is the nature of most metals — they combine with chemicals in the air or earth to create metallic compounds on their surface. We all know a few of these: rust, tarnish and scale.

Throughout the millennia, jewelers, blacksmiths and sculptors have developed exotic means to achieve patinas on metal. Modern chemistry has clarified the factors involved to the point where Theopholis' suggestion, written in the 15th century AD, seems, shall we say, quaint.

> *Working with care and cleanliness, mix equal parts of oil of tartare with cow dung that has been dried and finely divided. Mix to a paste with water or urine and apply with a brush made of the hair of a horse's tail.*

Technique aside, these instructions point to the importance of color on metal long ago. For centuries, color was more or less confined to patinas on vessels and enamels on jewelry. The past four decades have witnessed an exciting freedom in the use of color in metalwork.

The American studio craft movement traces its origins to the years immediately following World War II. Young G.I.s returned from their time overseas with new ambitions and a restlessness that made it difficult to resume the lives that had been interrupted. Many turned to working with their hands, where the immediacy of the results and the independent lifestyle struck a welcome chord. Ceramics at that time often echoed the hectic energy of Abstract Expressionism, and woodworking took cues from the highly refined elegance of Scandinavian and Japanese design.

Metalwork of the era was almost entirely in silver, either polished to a high shine or buffed to a soft matte finish. These finishes best complemented the sleek unadorned forms that came to be known collectively as Danish Modern. Attracted to this style, a generation of newly trained craftspeople arose, unencumbered by the family traditions of European companies or restrictive aesthetic ideas. The exciting work of these artists in the 1950s and 1960s helped to inform an interested viewing public. Through exhibitions, galleries and magazines (for instance, the new magazine *Craft Horizons,* later to become *American Craft*), a small but dedicated group of collectors began to coalesce.

In addition to studio work, many of these diversely talented metalsmiths also taught at colleges, in many cases forming metalsmithing departments where none had existed before. They created a next generation to whom the torch could be passed. To their great credit, this first generation did not restrict their students to the established styles of the past, but urged them toward new frontiers.

In the late 1960s and the 1970s, American crafts experienced a tremendous burst of energy and growth. Political and cultural changes led people away from the corporate suburban lives of their parents to experiment with alternative lifestyles. Colleges, workshops and a growing number of craft fairs facilitated the exchange of ideas. In a decade of Woodstock, Warhol and Watergate, elegant forms in polished silver seemed out of touch. The new generation turned to found objects, base metals and a "however-you-can-get-it" attitude about color. In a real sense, that is where our story begins.

In this book, we divide the complex world of color on metal into four families, aware from the outset that the categories will cross and mingle. This introduction will set the stage by offering an overview and description of each of these groups — patinas, enamels, paints, and the inevitable "other" category that we have cunningly called Avant-Garde.

While the intention here is not to get too technical, an understanding of the physics of color seems central to what follows. In an article in *Scientific American* (October 1980), Kurt Nassau explained it this way:

> *Interference (color) is often observed in thin transparent films, where part of the light is reflected by the first surface and part by the second. Whether the beams reinforce or cancel depends on the nature and thickness of the film, on the angle of the reflection and on the wavelength of the light. If the film has a uniform thickness, different wavelengths emerge at different angles. If the layer varies in thickness, then at any given viewing angle different colors appear at different positions.*

Patinas

Traditionally, Chinese sculptors buried their work in the earth with instructions to children or grandchildren to exhume the work when the patina was fulfilled. Today, because of our familiarity with metal sculptures such as the Liberty Bell and the Statue of Liberty, we have an understanding of patinas that seems rooted in our awareness of metal and time.

According to the dictionary, patinas are "thin layers of corrosion, usually brown or green, that appear on copper or copper alloy, as a result of natural or artificial oxidation." (*American Heritage Dictionary,* 2nd Edition.) In the studio, patinas are usually created by immersing a finished object into a chemical bath or by spraying the chemical onto a prepared surface. In some situations, the work is confined in a close space, where a specific atmosphere can be created. Most metalsmiths would probably agree that an important aspect of patinas is their unpredictability. Though foreseeable in a general way, the effect of patina chemicals is influenced by the temperature, the shape and working of the metal, and the ambient atmosphere. Perhaps there is something in this inter-

In a simple patina process, a sterling cup is warmed under hot tap water, dipped into liver of sulfur, and immediately rinsed under running water. The warm-dip-rinse process is repeated several times to develop the desired color. Portions of the patina may be removed by rubbing the work with powdered pumice.

action between science and chance that draws us to speak of patinas as we would of characters we've known, calling them gentle, chaotic or muted.

Patinas were almost certainly the first form of color on metal since, unlike other treatments that require a technical process, patinas happen naturally. Natural patinas are the result of chemical reactions — typically corrosive, and most often involving carbon, oxygen and water.

In contemporary studio practice, most metalsmiths take a proactive approach to patination, mixing recipes culled from media-specific books and taking some control over temperature and environment. A simple patina can be applied by immersion, for example, in creating a black surface on sterling silver. As with all chemical patinas, the first step is to clean the surface well. Mechanical scrubbing or sandblasting is often performed, or the metal can be degreased with soap and water or a high-strength cleanser. The work is then dipped into an amber-colored liquid made by dissolving a pebble of liver of sulfur (potassium sulfide) in warm water. The reaction is nearly instantaneous; the silver turns yellow, then brown, crimson and blue in quick succession.

Many patina reactions move more slowly, taking hours, days or even weeks to create an intended surface. Typical of this class of patinas is the formation of a crusty green compound found on copper and copper alloys — a reaction that requires oxygen and time. This is called *verdigris,* from the French words for "green" and "Greece," in a reference to the venerable patinas seen on the sculpture of classical antiquity. In many cases the patina solution is brushed or sprayed onto a surface. The immediate effect is significantly nondramatic; the metal simply looks wet. The piece is allowed to air dry; then it is spritzed with more solution and again allowed to dry. As the corrosive reaction takes place on the surface, a skin of copper carbonate forms, creating a blue, green or brown layer of patina.

These two procedures — immersion and spraying — are probably the most widely used patina processes among studio metalsmiths. They offer a general view of the way artists reenact the effects of nature on metal that has been exposed to the elements.

Unpredictability is an essential part of patination. The fact that recipes exist, and have names like "Blue-Green with Brown Tones," implies a level of precision that is not the case. The condition of the alloy, the freshness and concentration of the solution, the humidity, and a dozen other factors all affect patina growth. An application method particularly in tune with this uncertainty is known as "sawdust patina" or, perhaps more accurately, "random contact patina."

In this process, a patina solution is mixed lightly into a dry, flaky material like sawdust, wood shavings, grasses, leaves or confetti. The medium is tossed with the solution just as lettuce is tossed in a salad, the goal being a thin and irregular coating of the liquid. A clean metal object is then set into a bag of primed medium and sealed for at least a day. Those areas of the piece that are in direct contact with the moist material will have a spot of color. If the surface is not matured, the piece can be reburied in the medium, and the package resealed.

Patinas can also result from heat alone, and again, the results will vary widely depending on factors such as duration, fuel, atmosphere and alloy.

Patina solution is sprayed on an object while it is warmed with a torch.

Left: In the "sawdust patina" or "random contact patina" application method, metal is buried in sawdust that has been moistened with a patina solution. It is kept in an airtight container for at least several hours and often as long as several weeks.
Right: Patinas are sometimes protected from exposure to the environment by application of a layer of wax. The wax is rubbed on lightly, allowed to dry, and then buffed to a warm sheen.

As complex and varied as each of these patina methods can be, the opportunities for variation compound when they are used together. In addition, patinas are often applied and then partially removed, adding richness and nuance to the color.

Enamels

Enamels are a form of glass that is melted and fused onto a metal backing. The ancient Egyptians, masters of glass, were among the earliest cultures to use enamel powders on gold objects. Byzantine goldsmiths advanced the art, both sharing technology with and borrowing it from the Far East as the trade routes to China were developed in the 11th and 12th centuries. Ecclesiastic craftsmen working in monasteries elevated enamel work to a high level of expression and technical prowess in Medieval Europe.

Enamels are ground from lumps of glass, either commercially or by the artist as a color is needed. Generally speaking, glass (and therefore enamels) can be made opaque, translucent or transparent through the addition of various metal oxides. Melting points and rates of contraction can be influenced by adding fluxes and other chemicals. This results in a broad palette for metalsmiths — a situation that is as technically demanding as it is exciting.

In addition to having a range of colors, artists can choose from the many ways to prepare a metal object for enamel. In the simplest, a form is created and covered with a layer of enamel. More typically, several layers are applied to create rich nuances of hue and value.

Enamels are available as powders, lumps and rods. They are identified by numbers and should be kept sealed against dust and moisture.

In a process called *basse-taille* (bas-TIE), the area to be enameled is given a texture that will show through a transparent or translucent glass layer. If this surface is created in such a way that the enamel layer can be of differing thicknesses, the result is a subtle transition of value similar to what we see when we look into a swimming pool as it goes from the shallow end to the deep end.

In a process called *cloisonné* (klwa-zon-NAY), compartments or "cells" are created on a metal sheet and filled with glass powder. The areas to receive enamel can be created by carving or piercing, but more typical is the use of a thin flat wire standing on its side to create the divisions between colors. This wire reads as a bright line in the final work, giving cloisonné an affinity to drawing.

Typically, cloisonné wires are bent with tweezers and set into position on a metal sheet that has been prepared by fusing a layer of clear enamel across the surface. The piece is set into a kiln at a temperature greater than 1300°F (700°C), and the base enamel melts, bonding with the wires and fusing them into place. The piece is removed and slowly cooled. Prepared, moistened enamel powder is then laid into place with

Toru Kaneko, untitled vase, copper, silver and lacquer, 13½" x 13½" x 4½". Photo by Toru Kaneko.

a fine brush. The powder is allowed to dry, and the piece is returned to the kiln, where the powder fuses into a solid mass. Because the fused glass takes up less space than the initial powder, the process must be repeated to build up sufficient volume to fill the compartments to the top.

In most enamel styles, once sufficient glass has been fired onto the metal, the surface is ground with abrasive stones to level it. This is done under water so that the grit can be washed away before it becomes embedded in the glass. To achieve a shiny surface, artists often follow stoning with a final pass through the kiln, where the glass becomes molten and flattens into a reflective surface.

Paints and Dyes

Unlike patinas — where the color is a result of chemical interaction with metal — paints and dyes come with color built in; red paint is red whether it's applied to paper or metal. Paint as decoration on metal is certainly nothing new, as Henry Ford could attest. Some of the armor of Medieval Europe was polychromed to increase the drama and ferocity of the tournament.

Examples of painted metal surfaces are all around us, from automobiles to office furniture. Advances in technology have greatly improved the toughness, selection and range of effects possible with paint. Because these often involve sophisticated equipment like magnetic spray devices and sealed spray booths, metal artists often turn to related commercial specialists for expertise. The same technology that makes a stovetop fashionable and a motorcycle unique can be used in fine art metalsmithing.

Enamel is sprinkled onto a metal sheet through a fine-mesh brass or plastic screen. When the enamel has melted and fused onto the metal, the piece is removed from the kiln with a long-handled fork. After they are fired, enameled surfaces can be smoothed under running water with abrasive stones.

Resins

Color can also be applied to metal by including the color in a coating layer of plastic. "Thermosetting plastics" are large-molecule hydrocarbons that can be mixed from two constituent parts into a material that hardens from a liquid to a solid. Plastics that were an industrial marvel not too long ago are now so familiar that we can buy them at the local grocery store. Epoxy is an example of a commonplace thermoplastic — and one that has been used effectively to add color to metalwork.

In most cases, color is added either by mixing pigments into the plastic while it is wet or by embedding a colored material such as chalk dust in the otherwise clear medium. As demonstrated in the third section of this book, resins are being used to create a wide range of effects in contemporary jewelry, from a sleek modern look to a coarse encaustic.

Epoxy is a familiar resin. Here, equal parts are mixed thoroughly to begin the hardening process. Coloring agents such as enamel powder or pigments can be mixed into the epoxy; in this example, the agent is shaved pastel. The epoxy is meticulously deposited into chambers or compartments in the piece.

Anodizing

In an electrolytic reaction, positive electric current is fed into a liquid bath at a pole called the anode. Negative current is run through a piece of metal immersed in the bath, called the cathode. This process is the basis of electroplating and electroforming, and makes possible two distinct coloration techniques, one that works by preparing a surface to receive dye and the other by creating oxide films.

A small anodizing setup for coloring titanium.

Aluminum is a lightweight gray-colored metal. When the metal is properly cleaned and immersed in sulfuric acid, the surface is converted to a semi-porous, nonconductive, hardened surface. If the aluminum is exposed to dye at this stage, the color is drawn into the honeycomb-like surface layer where it can be sealed by a follow-up immersion in boiling water or hot nickel acetate. Color can come in the form of fabric dyes, inks and a wide range of pigments.

Electricity is used in another way (the second kind of anodizing) to create color on titanium, niobium and four other elements known collectively as the "reactive metals." When heat is applied to these metals, it creates a thin oxide skin that refracts the light that hits it in such a way that we perceive a rainbow of colors. Because heat is quickly dispersed through the metal, colors derived this way are difficult to control.

In the 1950s, it was discovered that a low-voltage electrical current produced this oxidation layer, and that specific voltages will consistently yield the same oxide thickness and color. Twenty years later, this information, and the artistic potential behind it, found its way into metalsmithing studios.

In this process, the metal is prepared either by aggressive abrasion or by cleansing in acid. It is then immersed, completely or in part, in electrolyte — a liquid bath that conducts electricity well. Electric current is passed through a transformer that alters its wave structure from an alternating current to a direct current. This makes it possible for a second device, called a "current limiter," to reduce the power to the relatively low voltages used in this process. The electricity is turned on for a prescribed length of time — usually less than a minute — and the reactive metal blooms into color.

Recent Exploration

Our basic understanding of jewelry and metalworking has changed radically in recent years. We used to think of jewelry as small, shiny, and silver or gold. But today, jewelry and decorative metal objects are often made of base metals such as copper or steel, and they may incorporate paper, plastic or wood. Talented artists have responded to this freedom with energetic exploration of materials. Nothing is off limits in this search.

One avenue of this exploration is the use of found objects. Bits of painted tin cans, toys and other castoffs are used in jewelry, prized for their color and the history they bring to the work. Images are sometimes carefully recycled and other times ignored in favor of a graphic statement about color and pattern. These common — and commonly overlooked — bits of cultural debris are given new weight by artists who treat them with the attention usually reserved for gems and precious metals.

A sandblasted surface can be colored with pencils, chalk, graphite, pastel and similar traditional drawing media. Spray fixative seals the finished surface.

Another unconventional alternative for adding color to metal is the use of media usually reserved for art on paper — colored pencils, crayons and artists' paints are being used to create complex and subtle color effects on metal. Because the surfaces of these materials are relatively fragile, all the hammering, bending, soldering and finishing must be completed before they are applied. The metal is cleaned and given a tooth by roughening the surface with abrasives or by sandblasting. The colors are applied and then sealed with a clear plastic coating.

The writer of Ecclesiastes apparently knew a thing or two about metalworking. Here is his description of the work of a metalsmith:

And his eyes look still upon the pattern of the thing that he maketh. He sitteth his mind to finish his work, and waiteth to polish it perfectly.

The writer could not possibly have guessed at the delicious metalwork being done today, but we think he would embrace the vitality of the pursuit evidenced in the pages that follow. Today's cutting edge is tomorrow's expectation. Flip the page and see what we'll come to expect.

Claire Sanford, *Ikebana Vases*, copper, 6" to 7½". Photo by Dean Powell.

Patina is to metal what scent is to a blossom: natural, expected and essential. Most metals and alloys are perpetually involved in chemical reactions with compounds in the atmosphere. We can see this in a rusty fence, in a lichen-colored roof and in the nut-brown pennies in our pockets.

Facing page: Stephen Yusko; see page 18.

STEPHEN YUSKO

Stephen Yusko's process begins in scrap yards, industrial sites and farm buildings, where he scrounges for materials with inherent history. Ideas for many of his pieces take shape in these favorite places, as he observes the interaction of balance and tension, simplicity and complexity, and time and materials. Ideas about color often begin here, too.

On one of his frequent visits to a metal scrap yard, Yusko saw threaded steel pipes that had been mangled by the bulldozer that was pushing the parts into piles. Fascinated with the effect, he took some of the pieces back to the forge, where he re-created the contrast of found pattern and hammer marks for this piece.

In forging and forming steel, Yusko often uses textured hammers and stakes to enhance or tone down existing textures. The coloring process begins once the components are assembled and the detail work is completed.

Generally, Yusko's first step in coloring is to sandblast the metal to create a uniform surface. All surfaces are then wire-brushed by hand to develop a satin sheen. He uses light colors of oil paint to develop contrast in heavily textured recesses. Then, wearing a respirator and working either in a well-ventilated area or outdoors, he lightly heats the piece with a torch and uses a paintbrush to apply a diluted solution of ferric nitrate. A second paintbrush, with the bristles trimmed short, is used to scratch through the paint, allowing the acid to attack the exposed metal. Many applications are necessary, each treatment separated by at least five water rinses. Fumes from the acid make this a hazardous process, and Yusko warns that it should be undertaken only with strenuous precautions.

Once the desired rust/paint finish has been achieved, the piece is soaked in a neutralizing baking soda bath and is then rinsed in water. When the piece is dry, a Scotch-Brite pad is used to expose bare metal in selected highlight areas. These are darkened with a commercial gun-bluing solution, a step that requires additional neutralizing and rinsing. The piece is dried and buffed with fine steel wool to even out irregularities, and then dried further to remove trapped moisture. After an hour or so in a slow oven — approximately 300°F (150°C) — several coats of wax are applied to the finished piece.

SAFETY NOTE: Yusko's process releases dangerous fumes, so first-rate ventilation is important. The paper filter dust masks sold in hardware stores are not sufficient protection. Canister-equipped face-fitting masks and active ventilation are recommended whenever working around strong corrosives.

Stephen Yusko, *Threaded Box,* steel, 4¹/₄" x 5¹/₄" x 4¹/₄". Photo by Jeffrey Bruce.

BILLIE JEAN THEIDE

In Billie Jean Theide's work, color serves as a conceptual device as well as a visual quality. Her fabricated and electroformed teapots reference Western and Southwestern landscapes of North America through their three-dimensional forms, texture and color.

Theide achieves color through a variety of approaches, employing patina, enamel and paint singly or in combination. Patinated surfaces are sometimes smooth and pristine, sometimes heavily encrusted; enameled and painted surfaces are monochromatic, subtly blended or graphically rendered. Ultimately, it is Theide's intention to provoke a feeling of monumentalism in spite of scale, and to convey a sense of timelessness and mystery.

While her primary references are land formations, her forms are also reminiscent of flatirons, tugs, ironclads and Yixing teapots. In her latest work, which combines silver plate and fabricated copper, Theide creates hybrid teapot forms. This cross-breeding of contemporary and historical elements results in objects which are intentionally playful, peaceful and ambiguous.

NOTE: The handle and knob of this teapot are recycled from an antique silver-plated coffeepot made by the F.B. Rogers Company. The parts were removed from the collectible vessel and attached to a form very different from the original. The hybrid form was then electroplated, painted and patinated with several chemical treatments.

Billie Jean Theide, *Hybrid 1 (Rogers),* teapot of copper, silver plate, enamel and patina, 7" x 9" x 2¼". Photo by Billie Jean Theide.

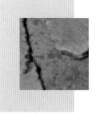

CAROL WARNER

Carol Warner has always been fascinated by the mysterious images of the ocean realm — from corals and tropical fish to the weathered, aging relics lost or left behind by mankind. As both a metalsmith and a scuba diver, she saw the similarity between the electroforming process and the growth patterns of coral. She now uses the electrolytic process to create in metal the surface quality of ageless underwater forms.

Using this ocean aesthetic as a point of departure, Warner ultimately strives to create images that display a classical sense of beauty, one in which surface quality and color enhance overall form. She adds color to achieve this goal, rather than to scientifically emulate nature's creations, often applying patinas to the inside of vessels, for example, to emphasize the relationship of interior and exterior.

Warner uses any materials and procedures that seem appropriate to re-create the visual qualities that she records in her diving adventures. The process often starts with traditional chemical patinas and is later modified with paints, stains, waxes and whatever else she finds to achieve the desired results.

In *Unearthed*, Warner has painted a chemical patina onto the interior surface to allow the bright turquoise to glow through fragmented openings of the vessel form. The viewer is allowed to glimpse a precious interior in the same way a diver catches quick peeks at delicate specks of beauty within an expansive reef system. Bits of the solution splash onto the vessel's outside surface, creating subtle variations on a seemingly natural, earthy exterior. By underplaying the exterior and placing the more dramatic use of color on the inside, she makes her vessel more sculptural and less of a utilitarian object.

Turquoise Patina
(used on the interior of *Unearthed*)
Combine equal parts copper nitrate and zinc chloride with enough water to make a paste. Brush a thick coating on the metal surface and allow to dry. Rinse with cold water and seal with acrylic spray.

Brown Patina
(used on the exterior of *Unearthed*)
Combine equal parts copper nitrate and ammonium chloride with enough water to make a paste. Apply, rinse and seal as with Turquoise Patina.

Carol Warner, *Unearthed,* copper, iron, patina and paint, 17" x 17" x 11". Photo by Warwick Green.

CLIFTON PROKOP

Clifton Prokop's artwork focuses on the relationship between nature and technology. He makes molds of images and found text; cast elements from the molds accumulate to become the patterns of his surfaces. Prokop's imagery seems accidental. In reality, each element is a reference to the continuum of time. After covering the entire form with patina, he polishes key surfaces to direct light — and thereby attention — to those areas.

Prokop begins the patination process by studying the surfaces and looking for a color combination of transparent and opaque patinas that will convey the elegant appearance of a historical artifact. He then cleans the piece completely by blasting with glass beads, handling it only with latex gloves; traces of hand oils might otherwise resist the patina. After this process is complete, he applies a base patina uniformly, rinses the piece well, and rubs selected areas with fiber pads to expose highlights and textures.

Prokop prefers hot patinas, and uses ferric nitrate and cupric nitrate over the base coat in combination with small amounts of other patina mixes, depending on the metal used. Each layer of patina is applied by brush or sprayed on, and then rinsed and reworked until the desired effect is achieved. While the piece is still warm, it is sealed with a light coat of Renaissance Wax. After it has fully cooled, each piece is buffed with shoe brushes to enhance the optical quality of the patina.

NOTE: Patination generally involves many repetitions. The metal is cleaned, and layers of chemical solutions are applied, rinsed and reapplied to develop interesting color. Layers may be partially removed or overlaid with other chemicals. When the color is complete, a layer of wax seals the metal against further corrosion.

Clifton Prokop, *Nature and Cyberspace,* iron, wax and patina, 10" x 6". Photo by Clifton Prokop.

J. AGNES CHWAE

In discussing her work, J. Agnes Chwae is quick to credit an influential book by Michael Rowe and Richard Hughes called *The Coloring, Bronzing and Patination of Metals*. Chwae uses formulas from this respected reference to color her work; the piece shown here uses recipe #3.137 for "Green and Blue-Green Patina on Variegated Orange-Brown Ground on Copper."

To color the bowl, Chwae dabbed the copper surface with a soft cloth moistened with the patina solution, and then left it to dry. This sequence of sparse application and periods of drying was repeated until the copper surface turned green. The patina was then scrubbed off selectively with a soft cloth to expose the orange-brown ground.

Over the years, Chwae has become familiar with many patinas and their characteristics. The results of some patina recipes are variable, while others prove themselves consistently reliable. Some patinas are very durable, while others are delicate. And some are altered over time by exposure to light.

As Michael Rowe and Richard Hughes state, "Coloring metals is not an exact science but depends to some extent on the skill and judgment of the individual." The artist agrees, but she sees in this situation an opportunity for spontaneity and surprise.

J. Agnes Chwae, *Aziyadé,* copper, 6" x 15". Photo by Jim Wildeman.

CHRIS RAMSAY

Chris Ramsay's work begins far from the studio when he collects objects at flea markets or on walks. The materials can be either man-made or natural, and are often aged or eroded in some way. He selects, organizes and inserts the objects into structures that have a form and surface related to the theme of the piece. In *Collection 1* he chose a circular form with a patinated surface as a metaphor for cycles of change.

Ramsay used Nazdar Screen Process Ink and 212 Blue Alkali-Etch Resist to silkscreen images of fossils onto copper sheet before cutting and forming the metal. He then etched the copper sheets outdoors in a child-size plastic pool containing three parts water to one part nitric acid at a depth of about an inch. He arranged the collected materials on top of the etched metal, paying attention to relationships between various objects and the surface images. The "editing" continued for several weeks, during which he shifted and reassessed pieces. He then pierced silhouettes with a deep-throated jeweler's saw to contain the objects, creating a unique burrow for each.

Ramsay first applied a patina to *Collection 1*. Dissatisfied with the results, he returned to the studio to do what he says he does best: experiment, discover and respond. Through repeated applications of the patina he was able to create a green outline in the lower portions of the relief and brown in the remaining areas: a result that was unexpected and exciting.

Blue-Green Patina on Brown-Black Ground

> 100 g copper nitrate
> 40 cc nitric acid (70% reagent grade)
> 1 liter water

Combine the ingredients. Heat the object with a blowtorch and apply the solution sparingly with a damp cloth or paintbrush. The liquid quickly turns dark brown on brass; on copper a plum color emerges. Persistent heating makes the surface blacken, and areas of blue-green patina begin to form. Continue heating and applying patina to establish a brown-black base and more evenly distributed blue-green. Allow the object to cool. Use water and 600 emery paper to remove patina from high areas. Rinse but do not dry the surface, and gently reheat the object to reestablish color in the sanded areas. Allow to dry thoroughly and seal the patina with wax. This semi-matte patina is especially effective on a heavily textured surface.

SAFETY NOTE: Nitric acid is very corrosive and must not be allowed to come in contact with the eyes, skin or clothing. Always add nitric acid to water (rather than water to acid) when mixing. Wear a face shield or goggles to protect the eyes from splashes of solution. Fumes released as the solution is applied to the heated metal should not be inhaled. Use adequate ventilation and a nose-and-mouth facemask fitted with the correct filter.

Chris Ramsay, *Collection 1*, copper, patinas,
fossils, shells, found objects and wood,
30" x 10". Photos by Chris Ramsay.

TORU KANEKO

Japanese metalsmith Toru Kaneko used a combination of repoussé and forging to create this vase from a thin sheet (0.5 mm) of copper. Repoussé is an ancient process in which the artist forces the metal into undulations by using a series of punches struck by a small hammer. It was chosen in this case not only for its visual effect, but because it makes the form rigid, giving it sufficient strength to function as a vase.

The surface color of this piece is the result of four distinct treatments. The silver-colored areas were plated by wiping molten tin onto the copper body. The golden part was made in a process called japanning, in which a layer of lacquer was painted onto the vessel and sprinkled with powdered gold while still wet. The piece was then heated to 248°F (120°C) to fuse the two materials. The blue section was patinated with ammonia, while the black at the mouth and on the repoussé was achieved with a sulfur solution.

Kaneko starts by analyzing the characteristics of the material he's selected, reflecting on its particular strengths and demands. This piece signals a move from the monochromatic work he's done in the past. As he says, "I feel confident about this direction, which allows me to go beyond the color of the copper alone by including other metals and their various color options."

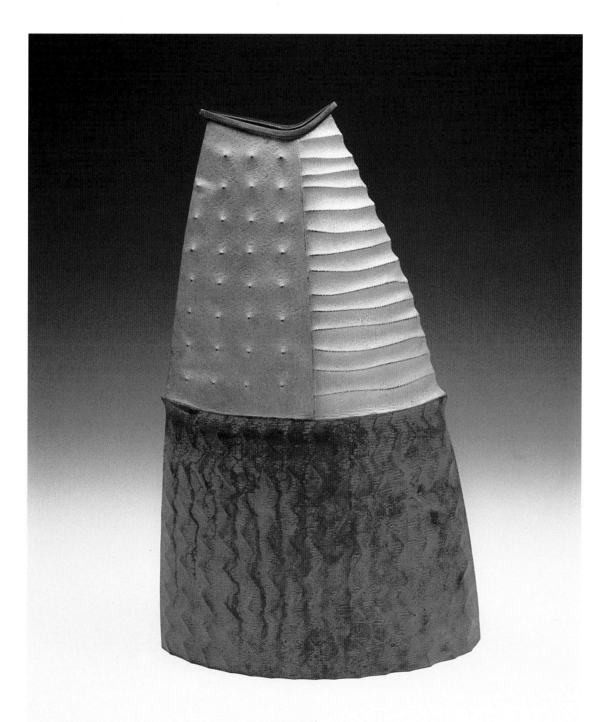

Toru Kaneko, vase, copper, silver, gold powder, tin plate, lacquer and patina, 12" x 7" x 3½". Photo by Toru Kaneko.

CHRISTOPHER ELLISON

Christopher Ellison would have been at home with the early alchemists, when earth, water, air and fire were perceived as the four and only elements. He begins his process by experimenting with the basic elements, and ends it with discovery.

Ellison views color as something latent, waiting to be uncovered to make the object complete. Relying on metal for his palette, he uses oxidation — the effect of air — to reveal the inner beauty of each particular piece.

The artist approaches both the form and his studio process with rudimentary and primitive energy. He grinds cupric nitrate and other patina chemicals with a mortar and pestle and mixes intuitively, bound by no recipe, comfortable with the honesty of trial and error. His goal is to instill in the object qualities of utility, antiquity and spirituality.

Ellison turns to the natural world for the finishing touches that he feels are needed to complete his work, making allies of time and the elements. He leaves his work outdoors for at least a month to complete the finish. Outside his studio in upstate New York, iron-rich rainwater creates trails through the brilliant copper blues. Meanwhile, the oxides continue to consume the surface metal, creating a constantly evolving work. Though he will occasionally seal a patina, Ellison's preference is to allow the natural process to continue. As he says, "Although we may feel we can alter time, it cannot be separated from the natural world, for nature works in concert with time."

Christopher Ellison, *Basket with Barbed Wire,* brass and barbed wire, 13" x 18" x 18". Photo by Christopher Ellison.

LYNNE HULL

Moss greens and deep-water blues characterize the Pacific Northwest. Lynne Hull, a native of the Puget Sound region, is naturally drawn to the similar colors of metal oxide coatings. She conveys the feel of the outdoors, spraying chemicals to speed up the natural oxidation or burying her lathe-turned objects in chemically dampened sawdust. An example can be seen in *Basket #23*, which was wrapped in an ammonia-soaked cloth and covered for 48 hours. When the patina was richly established, the basket was unwrapped and rinsed in cold water. After the piece dried, Hull sealed the surface with lacquer to create the characteristic depth of a patina.

Hull enjoys the contrasting interplay between nature and man, and sometimes uses auto paints along with her patinas. With *Purse Form* — a painted spun-aluminum vessel embellished with dyed nylon rods — natural and industrial processes collide. After the precise mechanical spinning was completed, Hull gave the object a gentle fold, before sandblasting it and painting it with flat black automotive lacquer.

NOTE: Spinning is a process in which a motorized lathe is used to create vessels. A turned wooden form equivalent to the inside of a bowl is mounted on a lathe, and a disc of metal is lightly pressed against it at the center point. With the lathe spinning, a blunt steel tool is used to press the metal against the form.

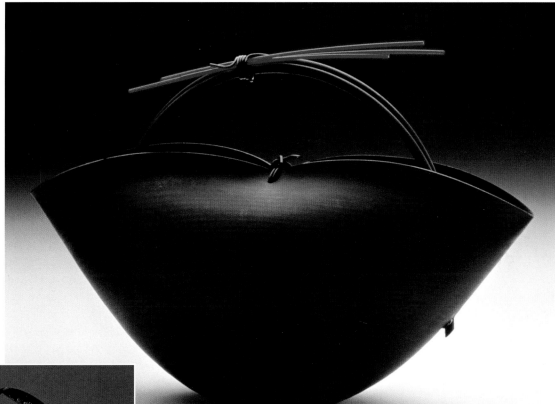

Above: Lynne Hull, *Purse Form*, aluminum, paint and dyed nylon, 9" x 13".

Left: *Basket #23,* patinated copper, 17" x 11" x 11". Photos by Kevin Latona.

ENAMELS

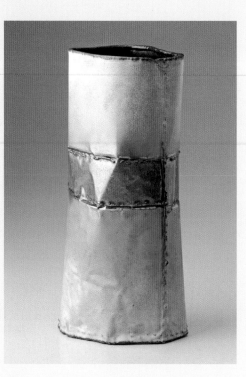

Certainly glass is one of the wonders of the world. It is mostly sand, but when mixed with a few other simple ingredients and heated to a high temperature, it can become vibrantly colored, transparent and reflective. Glass in the form of enamel has captivated metalworkers for at least two millennia — it is simultaneously familiar and spectacular.

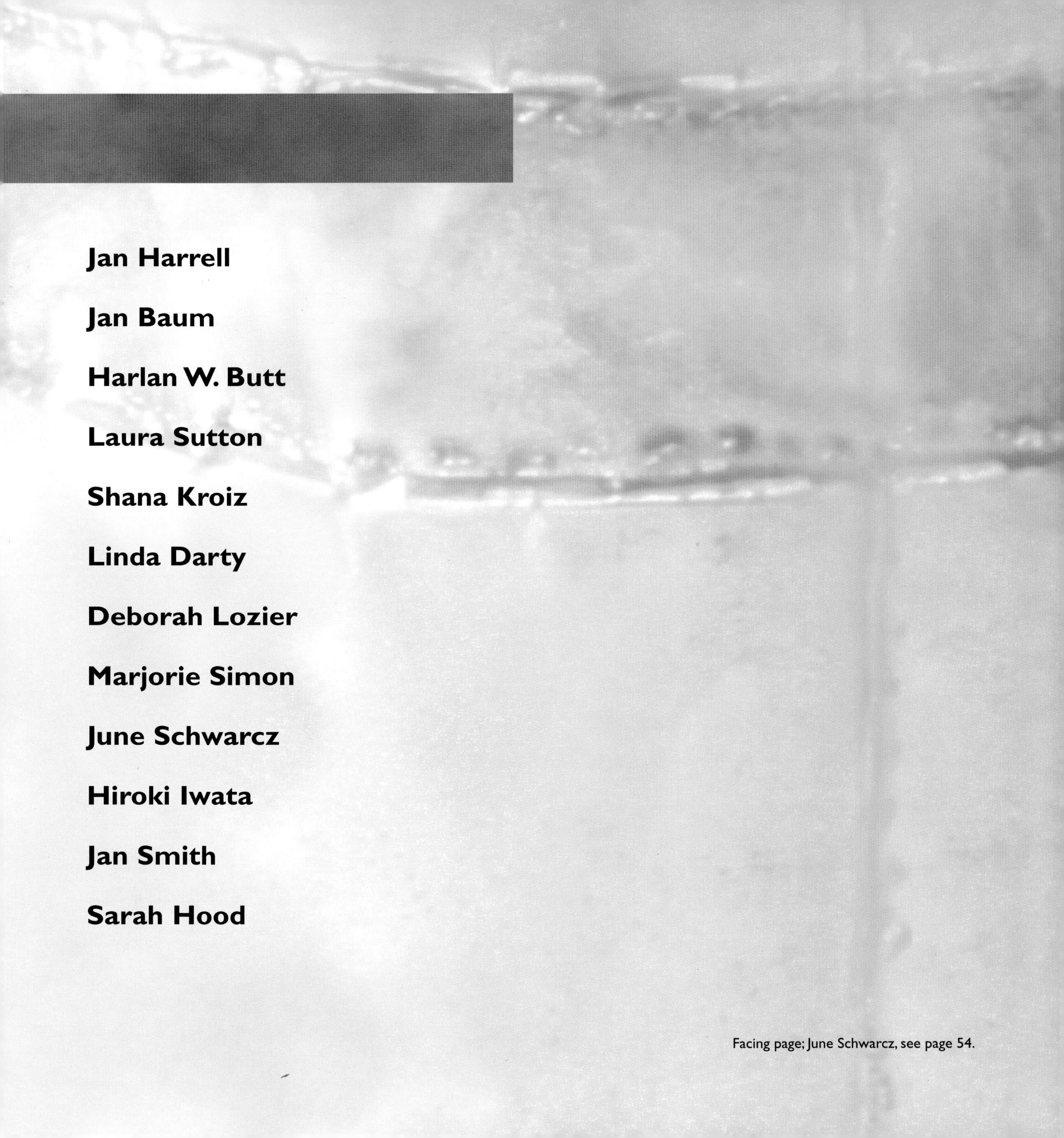

Jan Harrell

Jan Baum

Harlan W. Butt

Laura Sutton

Shana Kroiz

Linda Darty

Deborah Lozier

Marjorie Simon

June Schwarcz

Hiroki Iwata

Jan Smith

Sarah Hood

Facing page; June Schwarcz, see page 54.

JAN HARRELL

Since her first firing in an art class at a Texas high school, Jan Harrell has been addicted to enameling. And while historical enameling employs controlled and exacting techniques, Harrell seeks an effect that's less pristine, less precious. She wants the people who see her work to enjoy the colors without being distracted by the technical mastery required by the enameling process.

Copper, not the traditional bases of silver or gold, provides a first step in making this happen. Harrell says, "The colors produced when the enamels are fused on copper are warm and rich. The copper oxides trapped between the layers of glass create colors unlike any I could have thought up — a gift of the enamel goddesses!"

Calling on her background in metals, Harrell creates the enameling base by etching with ferric acid. Typically, she uses 16-gauge copper to ensure crisp edges and sufficient thickness to allow deep etched channels. She layers thin coats of wet enamels on the metal — an ancient technique known by its French name, *champlevé*. The process of building up colors and firing in between packings creates depth and matures the enamel. At least four to six firings are needed. When the recessed areas are almost filled with glass, Harrell must decide whether to leave the raised, exposed copper and apply a patina, or cloak the entire piece under a layer of transparent enamel. Regardless of the choice, she dulls the shiny finish by applying Armour Etch, a mild hydrofluoric acid paste. This creates a visual depth in the final piece unlike the reflective shine of heat-polished enamels. It also assures that the enameling process remains secondary to the color effect.

Jan Harrell, *Joy Luck Club,* enamel, polymer clay, sterling and copper, 3" x 1 $\frac{1}{2}$" x $\frac{1}{2}$". Photo by Jan Harrell.

JAN BAUM

Artist and jeweler Jan Baum has always been attracted to and intrigued by jewelry that functions as a wearable container. Using the formats of lockets, pendants and wearable vessels, Baum engages decoration and ornamentation to convey relationships and an expression of the human spirit.

Color plays a prominent role in this work, providing opportunity for another layer of emotional expression and further enhancing the complex forms. Baum's work draws broadly on visual sources such as Moorish design and architecture, Spanish aesthetics, accordion music and the work of Henri Matisse. She is also influenced by the theories of Susanne Langer, the phenomenologist and philosopher. Langer says about decoration, "Its office is to not only indulge perception but to impregnate and transform it."

Baum's approach to color is both intuitive and studied. Listening to the images and patterns as they develop, she renders pieces in white and then black, later arriving at the color palette. The colors and pattern are refined by repetition and an exploration of various methods of execution, texture and value.

Technically, the incorporation of color within Baum's work is accomplished through a variety of media. With *100% Pure,* she used china paints and vitreous enamels, as well as a ready-made painted tin as a decorative inspiration. By creating multiple layers — wearable vessel, container, color and pattern — Baum invites interaction and dialogue.

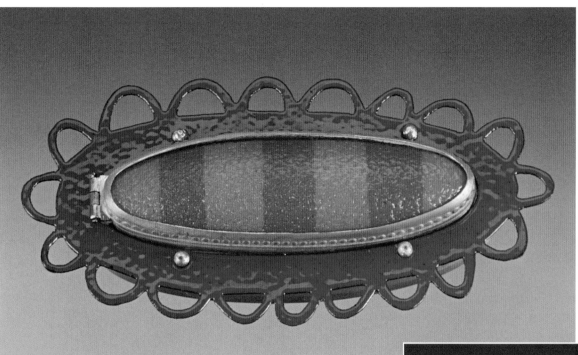

Jan Baum, *100% Pure,* sterling silver, enamel, copper, found tin and stainless steel, 2³⁄₄" × 1³⁄₈" × ¹³⁄₁₆". Photos by Bill Bachhuber.

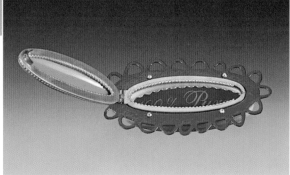

HARLAN W. BUTT

For Harlan W. Butt, color is a subjective experience. "I associate color and light with place and time. Gray-green: summer spruce in the San Juan Mountains. Vermilion and cobalt: Indian paintbrush and bluebonnets along Texas highways. Scarlet: autumn sunshine through Japanese maples. Color can also elicit mood and emotion. Cool and warm colors refer less to temperature than to the feelings they evoke. To me, they are stimulating or soothing, passionate or austere. The emotional impact of color can be used to create drama — for surprise or emphasis, metaphor or analogy."

Most of Butt's color is applied through enameling. Enamel can be opaque or transparent, glossy or matte, thin and filmy or thick and dense. In *Pumpkin Vessel,* this membrane of color simulates the actual rind of a pumpkin. The raised copper sphere was shaped to define the sectional character of a pumpkin, and then coated with a yellowish-orange layer of enamel. The surface was then sandblasted to remove the glossy shine, so that it more closely resembled the texture of the fruit. The stem was constructed from copper sheet, textured by chasing, and then given a reddish-brown patina. The overall effect is realistic — except for the barely visible foot. Upon lifting up the vessel, a hidden, removable container can be accessed.

Harlan W. Butt, *Pumpkin Vessel*, copper and enamel, 6" x 6" x 6". Photo by Jonathan Reynolds.

LAURA SUTTON

Laura Sutton explores color through torch-fired enamels. She enjoys working with thin copper onto which she applies enamels by both sifting and painting. The power of her colors comes from the interaction of layered transparent and opaque enamels and the contrasting use of firescale. Torch-fired enamels evoke a deep, rich and sometimes luminescent color that is not easily achieved with other enameling methods. By torch firing, Sutton develops an intimate relationship with the color and form, and through the push-and-pull of color application, she leaves traces of the process.

Because she physically manipulates the color with heat concentration and spontaneously added layers of color, Sutton feels directly connected with the work. The number of firings, the color choices and the heat placement all contribute to the outcome. She points out the personal nature of her approach and says, "This is not a formal enameling technique. I feel as if I take an alchemist's approach by exploring and transforming the enamel."

Improvisation is an essential part of the process. She explains, "My *Birdhouse* series is a journey of color and form. The rustic and weathered colors were inspired by my farming roots, while the vibrant hues refer to the stories that dance in my head. There is a sense of the uninhibited moment that allows my journey to continue."

NOTE: "Firescale" refers to an oxide layer created when certain metals are heated. These layers are typically something to be avoided or removed in metalsmithing, but Sutton uses them to enhance the effect of her colors. Copper is highly reactive with oxygen and creates several hues of oxide that run from red to gray to blue-black.

Laura Sutton, *Two Birdhouses* (detail), sculpture, copper foil and enamel, 10" x 5" x 5".
Photo by Russell Sutton.

SHANA KROIZ

Through her work, Shana Kroiz seeks a universal language. "My hope is that the work I create has the ability to communicate with all people regardless of their social, racial and cultural backgrounds," she says. The forms she uses for her brooches are based on a universal vocabulary inspired by shapes and motions that are common to all people. The work is therefore fundamentally comfortable to the viewer and the wearer. Inspired by the human figure and simple hand tools such as the axe and the arrow, Kroiz's pieces elicit a response that originates on a deeply personal level.

"My process of creation is one of development, reduction and embellishment. After the essential shapes are created, I minimize them into what I consider to be their purest elements," Kroiz says. She uses a die-forming process with a hydraulic press to mold her carefully planned forms in copper. Then she begins what she considers the intuitive part of their creation — the point at which the artist breathes life into the work.

Kroiz's brooches are first enameled with an undercoat of a solid opaque color and then tiled with shards of prefired enamel. They take on rich mosaic textures and colors that inspire thoughts, memories and emotions such as innocence, loss, excitement, confidence, sensuality, danger and joy. Each piece is a new step in an evolution that explores areas of the human consciousness that tie us together.

NOTE: A hydraulic press consists of a car jack mounted within a hefty steel frame that is in turn mounted on a sturdy table. When the jack is pumped, the ram drives against the frame, compressing dies and the sheet trapped between them. The device can deliver up to 5,000 pounds of pressure per square inch, allowing artists to create consistent volumetric forms quickly and easily.

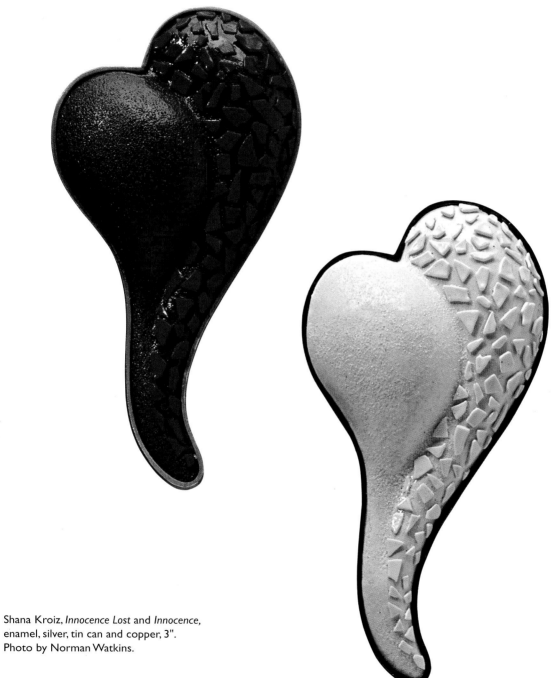

Shana Kroiz, *Innocence Lost* and *Innocence,*
enamel, silver, tin can and copper, 3".
Photo by Norman Watkins.

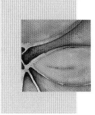

LINDA DARTY

Linda Darty's metalwork arises directly from the journal in which she records important moments in her life — times, places and people that she celebrates. Though taken out of the context of utility, her work is tied to function and strives to create poetic associations in an everyday setting.

The most recent series of pieces was made as a tribute to Darty's mother. "They evoke the glorious gardens and the flowers that I am surrounded by in my memories from childhood," Darty says. The artist cites vivid recollections of making flower arrangements and following her mother through the garden cutting roses and ferns. Even as an adult, when she needs a dose of calm in the chaos of her own life as a parent, Darty is drawn to the outdoors and the floral inspirations of her backyard garden.

Color is integral to this imagery, and Darty strives to reproduce the delicate subtleties as well as the colorful boldness of nature. Incorporating her love of drawing on metal surfaces, Darty most often uses the *champlevé* enameling technique, etching 14-gauge sterling before forming the pieces. Using mostly transparent enamel colors, she paints delicate hues in many layers with multiple kiln firings. When more appropriate to the design, Darty simply sifts gradated layers of opaque and transparent color on copper or fine silver forms. The velvety matte finish on the pieces enhances the incomparable luminosity and depth of the colored glass.

Linda Darty, *Garden Candlestick*, sterling and enamel, 4" x 3" x 3". Photo by Henry Stindt.

DEBORAH LOZIER

Deborah Lozier is a process-oriented artist who "listens" and reacts to her materials as she works. Her pieces are structured from copper, and colored with combinations of enamels and patinas, which she applies with the assistance of a torch. She tries to set aside preconceived images of what the finished piece might look like, and instead contemplates the results of each step to coax her pieces in a pleasing direction. And although forms and colors evolve as she works, she never considers them accidental.

The decision to torch-fire the enamel is based on her attraction to weathered surfaces as well as her desire for a direct relationship with the process. The painterly enamel effect diffuses into the oxidation colors created as the copper is heated.

For Lozier, the process of developing the surface is more subtle and quiet than the discipline of forming shapes. Meditating on the color choices is a place to start, but creating the desired effects in enamel and copper requires a different sensibility. The designing dialogue is ongoing, and a wide margin is left open for the materials to surprise and reveal their secrets. She confesses her addiction to discovery and is amazed by artists who can completely design a piece from start to finish before any of the work has begun. Lozier says, "I don't think I would have the motivation to begin if I were always certain where things might lead."

Lozier uses industrial objects as visual templates from which her designs emerge. This brooch is a translation of the sink drain in her studio.

Deborah Lozier, *Utility Brooch #2*, enamel and copper, 3" x 3" x ¼". Photo by E. Sarto.

MARJORIE SIMON

Marjorie Simon began using enamel as a way to put a durable coating of color on a three-dimensional object. Her current work emerged out of two simultaneous impulses. In 1995, Simon's travels to Europe and the Middle East included a visit to the British Museum, where a collection of 4,000-year-old Egyptian glass jewelry showed the colors of lively little flowers and fruit still fresh and bright. Then, in 1998, while recovering from a rotator cuff injury, she spent several months peering into her microscope, making detailed pen-and-ink botanical drawings with a clear reference to ancient floral motifs.

Simon knew she wanted the glass surfaces in this new body of work to look old, the color to bleed through and the edges to burn out. In the beginning, she worked only with red because she knew it would burn easily; later she added other opaque colors. The surface of *Egyptian Flowers* has been matted with acid and the blackened copper allowed to show through as a line. The tapering tubes have been textured with etching, roller printing or coarse files. Flowers are cut and sawn from sheet, domed in a die and manipulated by hand to achieve the desired "drape" or closure. The pistils and stamens are assembled from pearls and glass beads Simon collected in Murano and Morocco.

Marjorie Simon, *Egyptian Flowers*,
vitreous enamel, copper and pearls, 24".
Photos by Ralph Gabriner.

JUNE SCHWARCZ

June Schwarcz's vessels begin as panels of thin copper foil. Often, several parts are sewn together with fine copper wire, and then the whole piece is electroformed. In this process — an extension of plating — microscopic layers of metal are pulled from an ionic solution and deposited onto the form. The metal form is immersed into an electrolytic bath, a liquid that is especially conductive. As low-voltage electric current is run through the copper-rich solution, ions of copper are deposited onto the metal surface. The result, which is achieved slowly, is reminiscent of sedimentation or accretion in nature. It usually takes four days until the copper is of sufficient thickness to stand up to handling and firing in the enamel kiln.

Schwarcz achieves color with several layers of vitreous, lead-bearing enamel, and each vessel requires many firings in the kiln. In each case, sifted glass powders are meticulously dusted over the dampened surface and allowed to dry. The vessel is then set into a glowing kiln, where it remains, carefully observed, for several minutes until the glass melts into a viscous layer that bonds onto the metal.

Schwarcz uses mostly transparent enamels, though translucent and opaque varieties are sometimes used for special effects. Occasionally the vessels or the edges of the vessels are plated with a detail of gold, silver or iron.

June Schwarcz, *#2063*, copper and enamel, 10¾" x 5¼" x 3½". Photo by M. Lee Fatherree.
From the collection of Diana Munk.

HIROKI IWATA

Japanese artist Hiroki Iwata has recently turned to enamel as a medium for expressing imagery of the natural world. His starting point lies with the techniques he employs. As he says, "Clues that can trigger my imagination often lie hidden in process. In the case of this vase, I came up with a method I could use as a means of expression."

After building the vase form shown here with traditional metalsmithing techniques, Iwata fired a layer of enamel onto the surface. He applied gold leaf to the enamel with a diluted water-based adhesive and allowed the piece to dry. It was then fired in a kiln at 1364°F (740°C). To achieve the texture on the gold portion, he applied a thin layer of clear lacquer over the fired gold leaf.

The vertical stalk was also created with enamel. After firing uneven enamel stripes, Iwata filled the sunken portions with thick silver leaf, refired the piece, and polished it.

The piece shown here emphasizes elements of the natural world that softly embrace us all. Iwata started by visualizing the processes and components of nature that are otherwise taken for granted. For this vase, he had in his mind's eye an image of the power contained in a seed and the drama implied in its germination — the potential in each seed for rich and abundant variety. He says, "I strive to give maximum respect to all elements in nature, including trees, foliage and landscapes, as well as to the full variety of colors and textures inherent in the materials I use in my work."

Hiroki Iwata, vase, copper, gold leaf and enamel, 14" x 7" x 5½". Photo by Hiroki Iwata.

JAN SMITH

Jan Smith produces works that are pieces within a series, articulating recurring themes through layers of color, marks and imagery. She explores the physical, emotional and spiritual journeys of our lives, often using images such as boats and leaves as metaphors for travel, both physical and seasonal.

Smith's background as a printmaker influences her treatment of the surface and use of color. Enamel and etching provide a vehicle to incorporate a drawing sensibility in the work. She says, "I am seduced by the layers of transparent color and their luminescence. The manner in which I etch the metal and apply the enamels in fine layers, reworking and grinding the surface, allows the image to evolve in a very intuitive way."

Recently, Smith has been drawn to the idea of presenting multiple brooches in a sculptural format representative of a quilt. Just as quilts are becoming appreciated for their aesthetic value apart from their function and are being displayed as paintings, she is exploring jewelry that becomes more than body ornamentation. While at rest, the piece is displayed within its own environment, hung as a painting or relief and viewed as an evocative three-dimensional image.

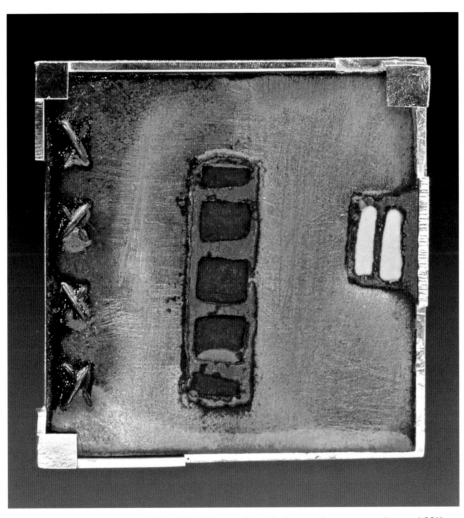

Jan Smith, *Brooch 5,* from the *9-Patch Quilt Series, champlevé* enamel, copper, sterling and 22K gold, 1 1/2" x 1 1/2" x 1/8". Photo by Doug Yaple.

SARAH HOOD

In her enamel series *Color Series: Dissemblance,* Sarah Hood scrutinizes the deconstruction of form and color. She considers both the minimum required to suggest jewelry, and the minimum required to evoke the natural world itself. Botanical structures are reduced to three-petal flowers and solitary leaves; jewelry is distilled to clean round shanks and simple connections.

By remaining elemental, these rings feel naive and pure — archetypes of natural forms. The brilliant colors present an image of a flower that is almost imaginary, yet somehow familiar, like a long-held memory from childhood. The color and stage of the blossom are frozen in time, ageless and never fading — a rendering of the impermanence of nature and of memory itself in a permanent way — an obvious fiction.

Because the forms are simple, color is the primary focus of each piece, but this simplicity is powerfully deceptive. The shocking red interiors defy the kindergarten quality of the exteriors, inviting the wearer into the raw, sensuous world that is the very lifework of a flower.

Hood works with enamels because they give a depth to the color that she can't get any other way, a fleshy succulence that belies the stiffness of the silver underneath and of the glass itself. She applies many unusually thick layers of enamel by dusting powdered glass inside and out, and firing until the flowers are plump with color, like huge jewels springing forth unexpectedly but without hesitation from the fingers of an equally spirited wearer.

Sarah Hood, two rings from *Color Series: Dissemblance,* fine silver, enamel and glass, 1 ¹/₂" x 2" x ¹/₂". Photo by Douglas Yaple.

PAINTS AND RESINS

The 19th century saw the birth of a new industry, synthetic dyes, which were developed to compete with naturally occurring colors. Since then, paints and dyes have reached into every aspect of our lives, from clothing to housewares to jewelry.

Jane Adam

Claire Sanford

Anne Mondro

Arline Fisch

Suzanne Donazetti

Susan Kasson Sloan

Linda Leviton

Reina Mia Brill

David LaPlantz

Jeffrey M. Clancy

Annie Publow

Katrina King

David H. Clifford

Facing page: Suzanne Donazetti; see page 72.

JANE ADAM

British jeweler Jane Adam works with anodized aluminum because it is light, durable and inexpensive, but most of all because of the freedom it allows her in making colors and marks.

Anodizing is an electrochemical treatment in which the metal becomes the positive element in an electrical cell, suspended in an electrolyte of sulfuric acid solution. Through this process, aluminum grows a thin, hard but porous surface layer of aluminum oxide that can be permanently colored with dyes, much like textiles or paper.

Adam's work centers on experimentation with what is primarily an industrial process, exploring its potential as a medium of artistic expression. She finds the possibilities it offers for mark making and coloration limitless and stimulating, and has amassed a huge repertoire of techniques. After 20 years of intensive exploration, she feels there is still much to discover. For her, the richness of color and effect that can be achieved turn this most commonplace of metals into a precious material.

These bangles reflect Adam's recent fascination with subtle marks and textures, and exploit the tendency of the colored surface of the material to crack when stressed. They were made from anodized aluminum sheet which was block printed with inks, immersion dyed, and sealed. The strips were then milled to stretch them — creating the cracks and the subtle crazed surface — and, finally, formed into circles.

NOTE: Block printing is a simple relief printing method in which dies are cut from wood, plastic, linoleum or rubber. Inks are rolled onto the raised portions, and then the block is pressed onto paper, fabric or, in this case, prepared aluminum sheet. With this step completed, Adam then dips the sheet into a vat of contrasting color to create patterns that are further enriched by rolling.

Jane Adam, bangles, anodized aluminum, 2" x 3". Photo by Joel Degen.

CLAIRE SANFORD

Color is key to Claire Sanford's work. In the brooches shown, she uses epoxy glue to capture and preserve materials within constructed silver frames. Earlier work incorporated unfired enamel powder as the colorant, while more recent pieces use botanical, edible or other natural elements for the color palette. For Sanford, sensory-rich substances such as spices, seeds, sand and hair have associations beyond the visual. She looks at them as being specimens from her life — in one way they become simple colors and textures, but at the same time they represent the things she lives with, cooks with or collects from the places she's visited.

Sanford's technique is based on cloisonné enameling, and allows for infinite variables of color and texture. Within a bezel-like frame of sterling silver, she constructs cells — or divisions — for each color. Working with strong ventilation or wearing a respirator, she mixes together equal parts of clear epoxy glue and then mixes in the coloring material. The piece is filled, left to set overnight and then wet-sanded to level the surface. To seal it, the epoxy is sprayed with Krylon Matte Finish #1311.

NOTE: Sanford prefers Devcon 2-Ton Clear Epoxy. She doesn't use Devcon 5-Minute epoxy because it sets up too quickly and can yellow over time. She says, "The colorant can be *anything*, so long as it's dry and doesn't have an oily base." Examples of colorants include powdered enamel, pigment powders, metallic powders, eye shadows, shaved pastels and spices.

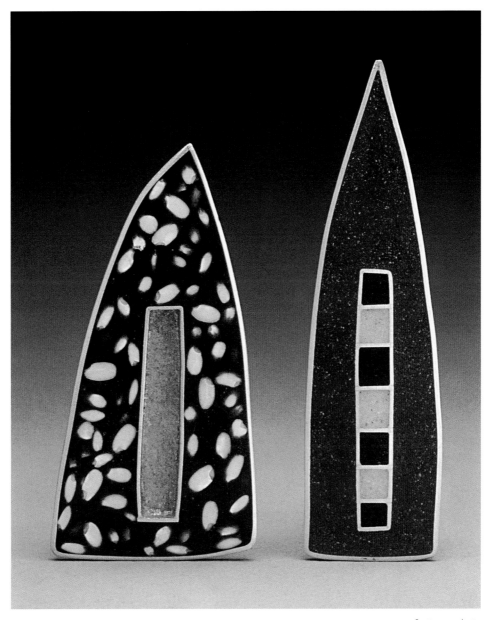

Claire Sanford, *Botanical Jewelry,* sterling, epoxy, cayenne, rice, charcoal and gold leaf, 3¾" and 4½".
Photo by Dean Powell.

ANNE MONDRO

Until recently, Anne Mondro's imagery was derived from colors and forms found in nature, especially the animals and plants found on the Maine coastline. Her newest work, the *Specimen Series,* focuses on the human desire to collect and display natural objects. Here nature is presented for analysis — the romantic view juxtaposed with the scientific view of nature. The forms Mondro creates are ambiguous; they refuse to reveal whether they are whole or partial, animal or plant, internal or external. The display of these forms is also ambiguous. They are bisected and presented for close examination, but they are also displayed in jewelry settings, raising issues of prestige and ownership.

Mondro uses the process of electroforming. She makes wax models and plates them with copper. The copper forms are then primed with gesso and decorated with oil paints to create a richly colored surface. Mondro paints the forms (as opposed to applying patinas) to prevent the specimens from resembling metal. Her color palette, consisting of red hues, also enhances the specimen's ambiguity. The color and the painted surface are integral in separating the forms from the structures that hold and display them.

NOTE: Gesso is a preparation of plaster of Paris and glue that has been used for centuries to prepare canvases for painting. It has the consistency of thick paint and can be bought at art supply stores. The bright white of a gesso layer makes an ideal surface for Mondro's brilliant paints.

Anne Mondro, *Specimen IV*, sterling silver, copper, gesso and oil paint,
2" x ¼" x 1½". Photo by Kathleen Browne.

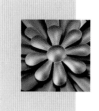

ARLINE FISCH

San Diego hillsides in the early spring are ablaze with flowering ice plant in purple, magenta, red, orange and yellow. The daisy-like flowers open in the sun and are absolutely brilliant by afternoon — a breathtaking view. They are so dense that all green vanishes and the flowers form a veritable Oriental carpet of color and pattern.

Arline Fisch finds the fully saturated colors of anodized aluminum appropriate to express the lush vitality of these exotic plants. Individual flowers are formed in a hydraulic press, using wires that have been bent into the desired outline. Thin sheet metal is embossed from the wire dies to create soft rounded forms. These are assembled into jewelry as simply and directly as possible, often using anodized pop rivets as the mechanism for combining elements. The puffed surfaces reflect light and color, while the layering of forms suggests the vitality of flowers moving in the breeze.

Fisch says, "I enjoy working in anodized aluminum because the coloring process relates to cloth in its use of pigment dyes. After the aluminum has been formed and anodized, the dyes are applied just as they are with fabric — by dipping, painting and resisting. In many ways, much of my work in metal is fabric related, and this dyeing of aluminum is a further extension of that interest."

It is important to the artist that the flowers be worn. They are not intended to be static objects, but to move with the body, to pick up changing light patterns and reflect the graceful energy of flowers. And they are meant to bring joy to the wearer.

Arline Fisch, *Layered Flowers,* anodized aluminum, 1" to 4". Photo by Arline Fisch.

SUZANNE DONAZETTI

"The excitement for me has always been working with color," says Suzanne Donazetti. She likes the subtle nuances of transparent inks and water on gilded copper and believes that color is a language all its own. For Donazetti, the experience of painting abstract designs on long sheets of copper is almost meditative.

For several years she used chemical patinas to color copper. Her dissatisfaction with the limited color range led her to experiment with colored inks and metallic leaf. With inks, mica powders and water, the colors, tones and hues are limitless. Throughout this process, she has learned the eccentricities of these materials and now uses watercolor techniques to paint directly onto the gilded copper.

Donazetti starts by gilding copper sheet with composition gold or silver leaf. Then she sands each piece lightly and lays out the sequential pieces (the warp beside the weft). After spraying them with water, she sprays or splatters inks that radiate into serendipitous patterns. She mixes mica or interference powders into the inks in abstract patterns determined by the gilding. When the various layers are dry, she applies paste wax to fix the colors and prevent oxidation. The final step is to cut and weave the copper in gentle curves and random strips.

Weaving the painted copper lends a refractive quality and adds a layer of mystery to her work. Donazetti says, "My goal is to learn about and to share this language of color in pieces that will give the viewer a chance to reflect — and feel the magic."

NOTE: Anyone familiar with the landscape of the American Southwest will recognize some of its qualities in the shifting light, warm colors and intensity of Suzanne Donazetti's work.

Suzanne Donazetti,
folding screen,
gilded and painted
woven copper,
54" x 72" x ¾".
Photo by Jerry
Anthony.

SUSAN KASSON SLOAN

Along with the "new" plastics, epoxy resin — a two-part adhesive that can be combined with pure pigment or myriad collage materials — was extolled as an artist's medium as early as the 1950s. It is practically indestructible and requires no special tools or equipment. Susan Kasson Sloan has been experimenting with this unique material since it was introduced to her in 1986, primarily because it offers a spontaneous approach to color. The relatively intuitive process she has developed has led her to a non-technical, painterly way of working.

Because epoxy resin is surprisingly lightweight, Sloan is able to work on a larger scale than she could if her pieces were constructed primarily in metal. She feels that larger surfaces allow more creative expression, and employs many familiar techniques of the two-dimensional arts, including drawing, painting and printmaking. She notes that the material handles differently as the viscosity changes with curing time.

The wonderful flexibility of epoxy resin as a painting medium allows Sloan to create whimsical images familiar from the paintings of Jean Arp and Alexander Calder. At the same time, the medium can be used to create frenzied masses of color comparable to the painterly styles of Wassily Kandinsky or Frank Stella.

NOTE: Resin is colored by adding dry pigment powders, available through art supply stores. Sloan finds that resins with a 30-minute curing time provide sufficient working time.

SAFETY NOTE: Resins contain solvents that can be dangerous to breathe, so ventilation should be used.

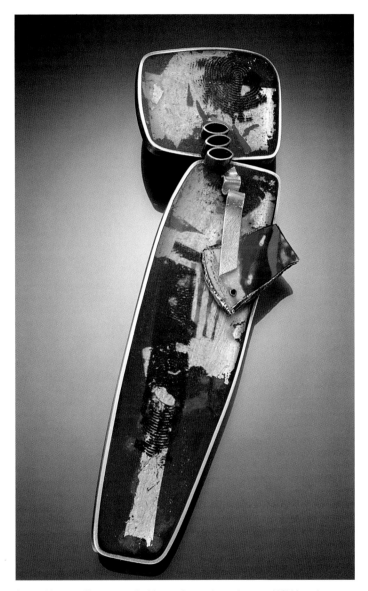

Susan Kasson Sloan, untitled brooch, sterling silver and 18K/sterling bimetal, 23K gold leaf and epoxy resin with pigments, 6" x 2¾".
Photo by Ralph Gabriner.

LINDA LEVITON

Linda Leviton makes sculptural works out of copper sheet and wire; these include quilts, fold-formed constructions, and woven forms such as this dress. She loves working in copper because of its malleability and because it can take on an infinite range of forms. Copper can also be patinated, painted and heated to achieve wonderful colors. At the same time — because it retains its shape — copper is amenable to many techniques, including weaving.

In this example, Leviton used a copper wire called "magnet wire," which she recycles from electric motors. This wire is available in a variety of vivid colors. It's easy to weave, and the resulting three-dimensional forms have a lightness and luminescence that is both solid and transparent, light and massive. Leviton works, life size, over a dressmaker's dummy.

Female forms and traditions often appear in Leviton's work. The dress and the quilt are historically acceptable feminine artistic outlets, but they are not typically associated with metal. "I use feminine forms but break tradition by making them from metal, a material associated with the masculine. Through careful color choices, I try to bridge the masculine metal and the feminine form," Leviton says. "Color adds an artistic and thematic dimension to my work, giving life to the idealized women in my *Eve* series."

Leviton's life-size garments use outrageous proportions: familiar, but not quite possible. Each piece becomes a character with its own personality, a whimsical play on female archetypes.

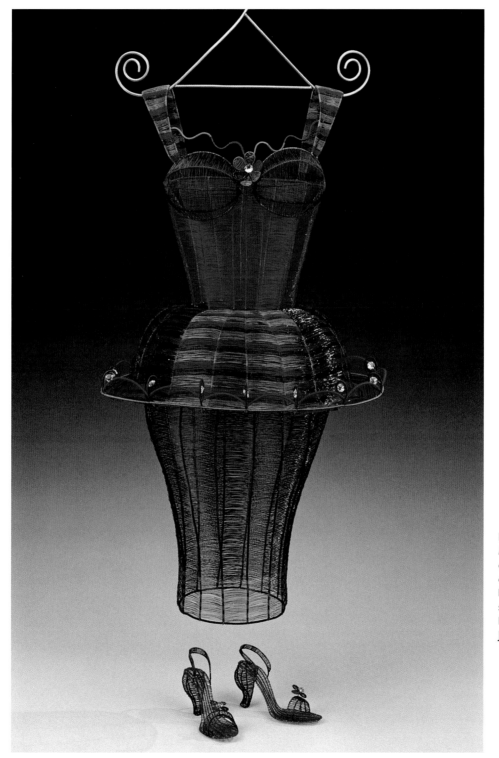

Linda Leviton,
Eve in Paris,
copper wire and
crystal glass;
body: 46" x 24" x 24";
shoes: 9" x 3" x 6".
Photo by
Jerry Anthony.

REINA MIA BRILL

For Reina Mia Brill, color brings life and animation to metal. It heightens the natural surface texture and adds tension to the work. Brill composes each necklace of formed copper mesh, either sewn or linked together with jump rings to allow for a sinuous line. All the pieces are painted after assembly is complete. Prior to fabricating each necklace, the copper mesh is annealed and pickled. Heating the mesh not only helps to soften it for shaping but also — more importantly — burns off grease or lacquer that would prevent the paint from adhering properly.

Brill paints each piece by hand, using a metallic acrylic paint. It is very thin — ideally suited for this work; enamel paint is too thick and has a tendency to clog the mesh. In order to achieve the desired radiant color, each necklace requires five layers of paint. The first three layers of base color — green, blue or pink — are applied separately and allowed to dry. The accent colors are added during the application of the fourth and fifth layers, while the paint is still wet. This allows all the colors to blend naturally into a beautiful palette.

Reina Mia Brill, *Petals,*
copper mesh and
metallic paint,
35" x 15". Photos by
Reina Mia Brill.

DAVID LAPLANTZ

The jewelry of David LaPlantz is designed and fabricated to convey the magic of horizontal layers, vibrant colors and ornamental textures. "My visual and imaginary world is similar to what one sees within the magic of a View-Master," says LaPlantz. "Each reel has two slightly different views of the same image, creating a very real, three-dimensional optical illusion."

Since 1980, LaPlantz has worked with the vibrant colors of painted aluminum, also known as "trophy metal" — the engraved nameplate portion of a trophy. He purchases these sheets of aluminum prepainted with vibrant colors. Starting with this basic material, LaPlantz exploits contrasts by engraving through the color layer into the silver-colored aluminum sheet. The freshness of the marks and drama of the contrasting colors creates a visual pizzazz.

In LaPlantz's hands, the layering of colors and shapes triggers an effective ornamental mechanism. He creates rich surface patterns by drawing grids, graphics, stitches, zigzags and lines directly on the metal with a steel tool.

For speedy, cold connections, LaPlantz uses HO Train scale iron nails as rivets. Their smooth, round black heads function as physical connectors, while also acting as raised accents or attention getters, defining the corners of a piece effectively and artistically.

"The uniqueness of the human vision and the way each human touches her or his materials — this is the magic that touches our hearts, minds and souls," says LaPlantz.

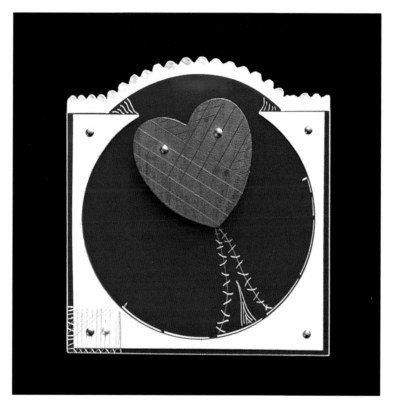

David LaPlantz, *Oh, Heart Face Brooch*, painted aluminum and wood, $2\frac{1}{4}$" x $2\frac{1}{2}$" x $\frac{3}{8}$". Photo by David LaPlantz.

JEFFREY M. CLANCY

For Jeffrey Clancy, metal alone does not always possess the visual strength he seeks in his work. This has led him to experiment with resins and embedded materials. He utilizes resin in a variety of ways to develop a wide array of effects. The well-mixed resin is colored by adding dry pigments, often in the form of powdered enamel — as in the work shown here. He makes numerous test tiles of varying proportions of pigment and resin to fully understand the possibilities. In this way, the same materials can create a smoky transparent effect or a saturated opaque finish.

Clancy also uses colored resin in an eggshell-surfacing process which is more commonly used in woodworking. First the eggshells must be cleaned by soaking overnight in a solution of 50% bleach and 50% water, and then left to air dry. He then applies a sufficient, even layer of an adhesive material. Although paste filler dyed with powdered pigment is normally used, Clancy prefers resin colored with enamel.

While the first layer of adhesive is still tacky, Clancy applies the eggshell in broken fragments with the convex side to the surface. He presses firmly enough to break the shell into smaller pieces, and uses a T-pin to adjust their placement. After the initial layer of pigmented resin has dried, a liberal second layer is applied to fill gaps. The work is cured overnight, and the surface is sanded down to reveal the fragmented shell.

NOTE: Clancy's process uses thermosetting plastic, a material that consists of two liquids — resin and catalyst. When the parts are combined, a chemical reaction creates large polymer molecules that harden into a translucent solid. Epoxies and polyesters are examples of thermosetting plastics.

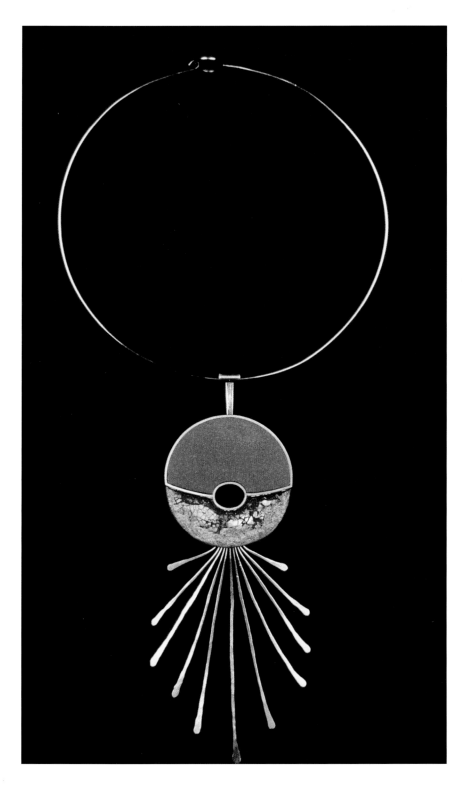

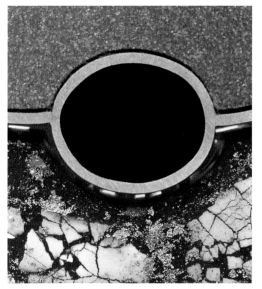

Jeffrey M. Clancy, *Round Neck Piece,* sterling silver, resin, eggshell and gold leaf, 14" x 6¼" x ⅜". Photos by Jeffrey K. Brady.

ANNIE PUBLOW

"Color is my first language. While I am aware of it both consciously and unconsciously, my experience of color is constant," says Annie Publow.

Though an interest in body adornment led Publow naturally into metalsmithing, it was only when she started working with aluminum that her love of both metal and color were finally in sync. Aluminum allows color to play an extensive role in her work because of the expressive palette available through anodizing.

Publow is inspired by color as a sensual property, one that must combine with other properties of form, texture and movement. From her first memory of light passing through a stained glass window to her current experience of her own metalwork, Publow sees the relationship of color with light as inextricable.

Much preparation is involved for color and light to play out their combined drama on the aluminum surface that is their stage. Only after a piece of aluminum is completely shaped, surfaced and anodized can it accept dye into the pores created on its surface. Publow dips the metal into dye baths and overlays colors with the aid of a paintbrush.

She says, "Though I usually have an idea in mind of the effect I'm trying to achieve, inevitably the coloring process is intuitive. The drama of applying color to a gray, anodized surface is, I must say, seductive."

The form for this pasta fork came from the idea of the stalk of a fanciful plant. Publow started by imagining a plant in a black-and-white garden; then, in the last step, she breathed life into the form by adding color.

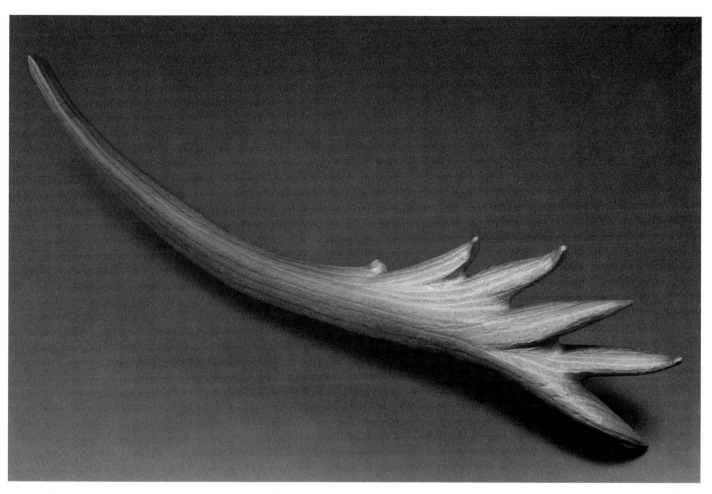

Annie Publow, *Pasta Fork*, anodized aluminum, 10" x 3" x ³⁄₄". Photo by Helen Shirk.

KATRINA KING

"Color on metal has always appealed to me, whether on an enameled object or a rusted piece of steel that still has evidence of the original paint," says Katrina King. Until the creation of her most recent body of work, King had used patinas as a primary source of color. But as most metalsmiths know, patina results can be unpredictable. In an attempt to control surface color, King began using colored pencil on top of the patinas, which were then sealed with melted wax, a technique known as "encaustic." This produced a rich, saturated and desirable effect. There were, however, only a limited number of colors she could produce in this way because of the subdued base colors of the patinas.

She began experimenting first with acrylic paints, which she discovered scratched off too easily, and then oil paints, which proved successful. Once King became comfortable with the technique of applying paint to metal, she took a closer look at what color "meant," and discovered that the commonly accepted theoretical and symbolic meanings did not match up with her own ideas. She arrived at her current palette via an intuitive process and says, "Color is a tool that helps me to gain more insight into a piece. It has given me access to emotions and intangible qualities that I could not express solely through the use of metal."

Katrina King, *Courage*, suspended sculpture, electroformed copper, nickel, fabric and oil paints, 6½" x 2". Photo by Katrina King.

DAVID H. CLIFFORD

Anodized aluminum has been reduced to a stereotype of cheap objects rendered in bright pinks and purples. In his work, David Clifford seeks to take advantage of the rich possibilities of this exciting process by using a wide range of subtle colors. He loves the idea of transforming lackluster, secondhand aluminum housewares into richly dyed allegorical subjects, while never losing sight of their intended function. Pictured is *Mentor, Friend, Father,* a commemorative trophy to his father. The pitcher is to be filled with beer (preferably Coors) to toast the son's appreciation of his father.

Clifford uses the sulfuric acid process he learned from his teacher, Thomas S. Brown, and from David LaPlantz's book *Artists Anodizing Aluminum*. He follows the process exactly as it is described in that book — save for a few rinsing buckets here and there. This involves roughly 20 sequential steps that include degreasing, etching, neutralizing, dyeing and sealing, always with several rinses in between.

To illustrate the rich tones of a Southern California smog sunset, and the warm and cool faded hues of flesh, Clifford begins by outlining his images on the aluminum with an engraver. The engraved lines later act as valleys to hold black paint; they add definition when color contrast is subtle. Using only five dyes — red, yellow, turquoise, violet and black —Clifford can achieve hundreds of hues, tones and values by dipping, stripping, layering or juxtaposing colors. Once satisfied with a particular color, he saves it, using a clear, fast-drying lacquer as a resist. Clifford completes the anodizing process in one sitting; any dust settling on the piece if left overnight might cause flaws in the surface.

Requisites for anodizing include adherence to safety, cleanliness, patience and an obsessively neat character.

David H. Clifford, *Mentor, Friend, Father,*
engraved anodized aluminum
thrift store pitcher, 6" x 12".
Photos by Thomas Brown.

AVANT-GARDE

Jewelry and metalwork have always played a role in fashion; they are at home with the avant-garde. Today's jewelers and metalsmiths are finding rich opportunity for colorful expression with innovative materials and techniques.

Mary Kanda

Ronald Lodes

Diane Falkenhagen

Harriete Estel Berman

Boris Bally

Marilyn da Silva

Robert Ebendorf

Helen Shirk

Teri Blond

Ivan Barnett and Allison Buchsbaum Barnett

Donna D'Aquino

Chris Lowe

Deborah Boskin

Nicole Bsullak

Thomas Mann

John Grant

Facing page: Boris Bally; see page 100.

MARY KANDA

Mary Kanda's jewelry consists of constructed silver forms inlaid with glass beads. The beads are fixed in place with wood glue, then the spaces between the beads are filled with tile grout. The claylike grout cement is pressed gently between the beads, which are then wiped clean with a sponge.

"The grout color has an enormous impact on the overall color and mood of the piece," Kanda says. "The aspect of my work that most fascinates and frustrates me is exploring various color combinations. Because it was difficult to anticipate how the grout would affect the piece, I worked with only black grout for the first couple of years. When I eventually began experimenting with other grout colors, some of the results were astoundingly ugly, but

I decided they were just 'unusual,' so I sent them out into the world. For the most part, I really wish I hadn't. Seeing some of those pieces again after time had passed, I wanted them all smote from the earth."

It has been several years since those experiments, and Kanda feels she is beginning to grasp the concepts of color. She has developed an inventory of grouted colors and is exploring "visual mixing," a process in which two colors, side by side, are blended in the eye of the viewer to create a third color. For example, when she surrounds an opaque yellow bead with blue grout, the effect is a green cast. Kanda's most recent work, which incorporates torch-fired glass elements and glass shards along with the beads, has emboldened the artist and re-ignited her urge to experiment.

Mary Kanda, mixed long- and short-leaf brooches, glass beads, silver, torch-fired glass and tile grout, 1" x 4¼" and 1½" x 2½". Photo by Dean Powell.

RONALD LODES

olor on titanium is produced by an oxide layer that forms when the metal is subjected to heat. Specific, controllable voltage levels develop oxide layers of consistent thickness. These layers refract light differently — an effect that reaches the eyes as a rainbow of colors. This process, called anodizing, is a richly colorful form of patination.

Ronald Lodes uses anodizing to color metal in his production jewelry, as well as his vessels and other large pieces. He employs three voltage levels to produce colors in varying ranges, and controls color placement through a painted "resist."

Lodes uses tape to mask selected areas, and then sprays high-temperature automotive engine paint over portions of the piece that will be anodized at lower voltages. After anodizing first at approximately 80 volts, Lodes removes the paint with lacquer thinner. This process is repeated, with the piece anodized at increasingly lower voltages. Anodized titanium can be sky blue, magenta, brilliant electric blue, vermilion, brownish gold and mint green.

The coloring technique used on this piece was done by setting the voltage initially at a high level (approximately 80 volts) and dipping the piece quickly, before it had a chance to fully oxidize. Consequently, the metal shows a transition of colors rather than just one particular hue.

Preparation of the metal prior to anodizing is highly critical. Lodes uses a hydrofluoric and nitric acid etch, followed by a baking soda neutralizing bath.

SAFETY NOTE: Like many high-tech procedures, anodizing involves potentially dangerous chemicals. In addition, electricity is used to activate the metal surface, so there is a potential for serious shock. Safety measures include wearing rubber gloves and apron, using eye protection such as splash goggles, and working with good ventilation.

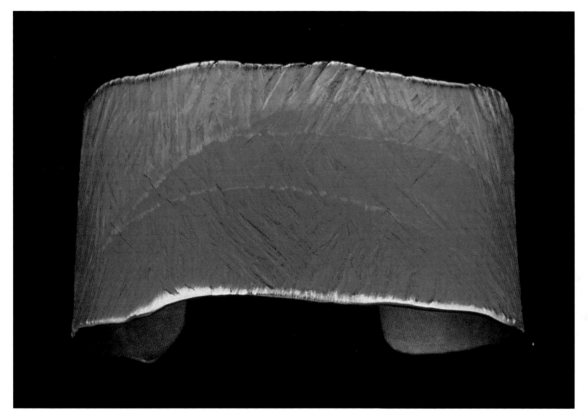

Ronald Lodes, *Rainbow Bracelet,* anodized titanium, 2½" x 2". Photo by David Durham.

DIANE FALKENHAGEN

One of Diane Falkenhagen's favorite pastimes is combing the aisles of hardware stores and art supply shops. Her fabricated mixed-media jewelry often incorporates unusual materials she discovers on these excursions.

Although narrative in nature, Falkenhagen's brooches are intended more to convey a mood than to tell a story. Whether the mood is one of drama, romance, nostalgia or despair, artistic and conceptual devices such as symbolism and color play an important role.

The pictorial tableaux in pieces such as *Scene From the Great Drama of the Human Race III* are borrowed from famous historical paintings. Using a simple transfer technique, Falkenhagen bakes printed images onto polymer clay, then manipulates them with colored pencils and seals them with polyurethane. For her metal frames, she uses traditional fabrication techniques combined with experimental surface treatments.

The luscious teal-colored surface shown here was achieved by applying a hard wax finish directly to the metal. Falkenhagen has experimented with various homemade formulas, but finds the easiest and most reliable results come from a ready-made product called Rub 'n' Buff. This is a quick-drying decorator's finish made primarily from carnauba wax, fine pigments and metallic powders. It comes in 18 colors and is available in most hobby stores. By mixing different Rub 'n' Buff colors or by adding additional dry pigment, an infinite variety of colors can be achieved.

Falkenhagen prepares the metal by sandblasting with a coarse medium. The wax mixture can then be applied thickly with a palette knife or thinly with a soft cloth. For specks of contrasting color in an impasto surface, she sprinkles chips of colored pencil lead over the soft wax and presses them in lightly with a palette knife. When the wax is dry, it can be burnished with an agate burnisher or buffed vigorously with a soft, lint-free cloth. The result is a rich and very durable finish.

Diane Falkenhagen, *Scene from the Great Drama of the Human Race III,* image transfer on polymer clay, hard wax, copper, glass and 14K gold, 3" x 2¾" x ¼". Photo by Bill Pogue.

HARRIETE ESTEL BERMAN

The colors, patterns, words and images of Harriete Estel Berman's work are carefully chosen from recycled "tin" containers. This preprinted steel is deconstructed, cut, folded and reassembled to contribute important content to her work. Cut with pinking shears, the material makes a sharp and pointed commentary about our consumer society — this metal is not as precious as gold or silver, but in many ways the patterns, words and images reveal more about the values of our society.

Making bracelets out of tin containers allows Berman to select a piece of material purely for its color or design. The different facets are never the same pattern; that would be too easy! Instead, the colors and patterns push and pull on one another, stretching a viewer's expectations. Still, they must work together as a whole, each side inseparable from the other. Berman says the selection of the colors and patterns is the most exciting and challenging part of constructing each bracelet.

Where does Berman find her containers? With some help from family and friends. "Actually," she says, "my father finds a lot of tins at flea markets, funky antique stores and church rummage sales on the East Coast, where the pickings are the best. Sometimes I get tins at resale shops or from people's recycling bins. After friends and acquaintances find out about my work, they give me cans — even my children's orthodontist saves tins for me. My studio is filled with hundreds of tins, but I always need more!"

NOTE: We often hear the term "cookie tin," though in fact these popular containers have been made of steel for the past 150 years. Paints are printed onto flat metal sheets that are then bent into canisters, boxes, toys and — yes — cookie tins.

Harriete Estel Berman, bracelets, preprinted steel and brass trim, 4" to 12". Photo by Philip Cohen.

BORIS BALLY

Until recently, color was not a part of Boris Bally's creative vocabulary; instead, he focused on form and composition. Although he found himself getting bored with the silver and ebony he was using, he was not drawn to conventional enameling or other traditional ways of applying color. Then, one day, he picked up a discarded traffic sign, became fascinated by the reflective, graphic-laden, weatherworn aluminum, and began a new body of work.

Bally's most difficult technical hurdle was to make this material wearable as jewelry. After trying several ideas, he designed a special swage connection to lock pinstems into the aluminum without the use of heat. The sign material is drilled partway through with a specially trimmed, flatter-than-usual, drill bit. A commercial jewelry finding is then seated in this blind hole. The finding is set, much as a precious stone would be, with a specially shaped hollow punch that forces metal fingers over the hole to permanently trap the finding. The edges are carefully sanded, and then the pieces are sealed with a coat of Armor All Protectant.

To maximize the sign imagery, Bally developed a group of archetypal, geometric forms. Using these templates, he playfully appropriates the ready-made graphics, selecting images and shades of patinated colors from the palette of his urban vista. The shapes are then extracted by sawing. Edges are carefully sanded and hand filed, and then the pieces are scrubbed clean and sealed. With a jeweler's touch, they become less recognizable and transcend their designation as scrap to become glowing urban icons.

As a reminder that these materials have been legally acquired and recycled from a variety of state and local departments of public works, the brooch series bears the standard abbreviation of *DPW*.

Boris Bally, *DPW Brooches,* recycled traffic signs, 3" x 7" x ¹/₂". Photos by Dean Powell.

MARILYN DA SILVA

"Color is an essential aspect of my work. It allows me to enhance the forms, distinguish the elements, set the mood and complete the story," says San Francisco Bay-area metalsmith Marilyn da Silva. Da Silva accomplishes this through the use of colored pencils and gesso — media she began to use in 1987 when, because of health considerations, she decided to enrich her surfaces with something other than chemical patinas. The move to pencils and gesso was a natural choice because of her strong background in two-dimensional work.

That decision proved to be a turning point in the artist's work. "I use gesso and colored pencils because they make it possible for me to maintain the 'presence' of the metal while controlling the placement, hues and intricacies of the color," says da Silva. "The application of this process is endless and as personal as the artist's own approach to drawing."

The Devil's Garden, which consists of seven large hat pins, has a rich and layered surface through a combination of heat patinas and rust, as well as gesso and colored pencils.

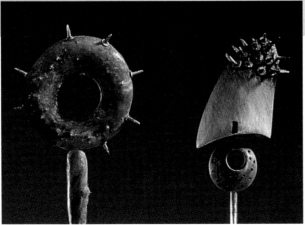

Marilyn da Silva, *The Devil's Garden*, copper,
steel, wood, lead, gesso and colored pencil,
13" x 16" x 4". Photo by M. Lee Fatherree.
From the collection of the Oakland Museum.

ROBERT EBENDORF

Robert Ebendorf is driven by the objects that he finds; they are a catalyst to his creative process. He becomes passionate when talking about the effects of time and place on objects. "It can be a piece of metal lying on the street, scratched and marred, with torn edges. Rain has created rust. It may be part of a broken tin toy found at the flea market or a crab claw discovered on the beach parched by the sun, losing the gift of color that nature has given it. To me, these materials are just as exciting and precious as diamonds and gold acquired from dealers."

The process of recycling objects has captivated Ebendorf for more than 30 years. Trained as a goldsmith, he uses his technical skills on ordinary objects to create what he calls "the sublime or the ridiculous." He has always been drawn to natural patinas or unusual surfaces that may appear on fragments broken from well-worn objects.

When a viewer looks at one of his pieces, the artist would rather hear a cry of "Oh my god, that is so ugly!" than a quiet expected response to just another piece of jewelry. Ebendorf uses his work to constantly explore the hidden language of materials. He hopes his pieces will engage viewers enough that they will join in his game — using whimsy and contrast to question the meaning of jewelry and personal adornment.

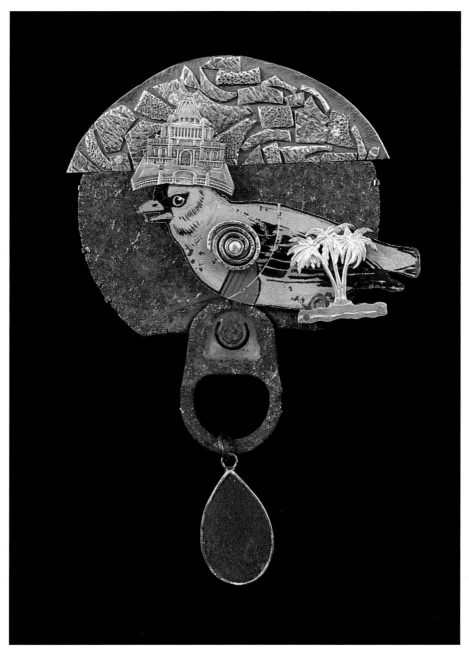

Robert Ebendorf, *Yellow Bird,* silver, tin, lapiz and 18K gold, 2½" x 3". Photo by C. Core.

HELEN SHIRK

Landscape imagery has strongly influenced Helen Shirk's hollowware in the past 14 years. The diversity of natural habitat and vegetation around her home in Southern California provides a rich resource from which she draws inspiration and meaning for her work. Her interest in brilliantly colored and textured forms also reflects the lasting impact of time spent in western Australia, one of the richest and most varied wildflower areas in the world.

Vividly colored plantlike forms emerge from the repousséd surfaces of Shirk's large copper bowls, or cluster together in freestanding groups that thrust themselves energetically into space. The contours, smells, sounds and intimate details of her travels emanate intensely from the walls of these pieces. Her recent series of standing cups and teapots stems from her respect for the history of functional objects as well as their potential to commemorate what she finds significant in life.

Always drawn to the challenge of physically manipulating metal, Shirk often repoussés spun copper surfaces with specially altered hammers to create an intriguing and seductively energetic natural world. She achieves a more aggressive dimensionality in recent pieces like *Commemorative Cup I* by building the piece part by part through the use of soldered construction.

After the form is finished, the piece is prepared for coloring by sandblasting with garnet grit. The next step, coloring, is central to the impact of the piece. Shirk employs a carefully chosen palette to evoke desired emotions while simultaneously visually manipulating the metal form. She uses colored pencils because of the range available, their blending possibilities and their ease of application. After the pencil application is finished, the entire piece is dipped in a liver of sulfur solution that blackens all uncolored areas of the copper surface, creating a crackled appearance and dramatically changing the tone of the piece.

NOTE: Sandblasting is a mechanical process in which particles are thrown against an object by a directed stream of air. For small objects, a gun-like device is used to direct the stream within an enclosed box. Particles can be garnet, which Shirk uses, or other materials including aluminum oxide and glass beads.

Helen Shirk, *Commemorative Cup I,* copper, patina and Prismacolor, 18" x 11" x 5".
Photos by Helen Shirk. From the collection of the Mint Museum of Craft + Design.

TERI BLOND

Teri Blond is fascinated with the appearance of iridescent beetles, and this fascination has led her to experiment with replicating the look on metals, using resin as a suspension medium and glaze.

She fabricated the piece shown and then used a procedure called "depletion gilding" to raise fine silver to the surface and prevent oxidation. The areas coated with resin are the eight segments below the five stones. On clean, unpolished silver, she blackened the center of each segment and outlined the outer portions using a fine-point Sharpie permanent marker.

Onto this base, she spread a layer of 330 epoxy resin. Because it is imperative to mix the epoxy well, she used a palette knife in a circular, lifting, smashing motion for 90 seconds to blend the two-part adhesive. She applied the epoxy onto the work using a toothpick and, while the resin was wet, sprinkled the surface with iridescent blue-violet medium glitter. The piece was inverted over a trash can to remove excess glitter. The blackened areas appear dark blue, while the bare silver areas reflect hints of color only as the light strikes from different angles.

After all the resin work was done, the piece was sanded with increasingly finer grades of abrasive papers. This process is done with water to minimize exposure to the dangerous dust that is created. The work was then dried and buffed with a clean muslin polishing wheel.

NOTE: Sometimes resin is sticky hours after it should have cured. This indicates that it was not mixed properly or not compatible with the suspended medium. To remove resin, soak the piece in Strypeeze Semi-Paste Paint Remover.

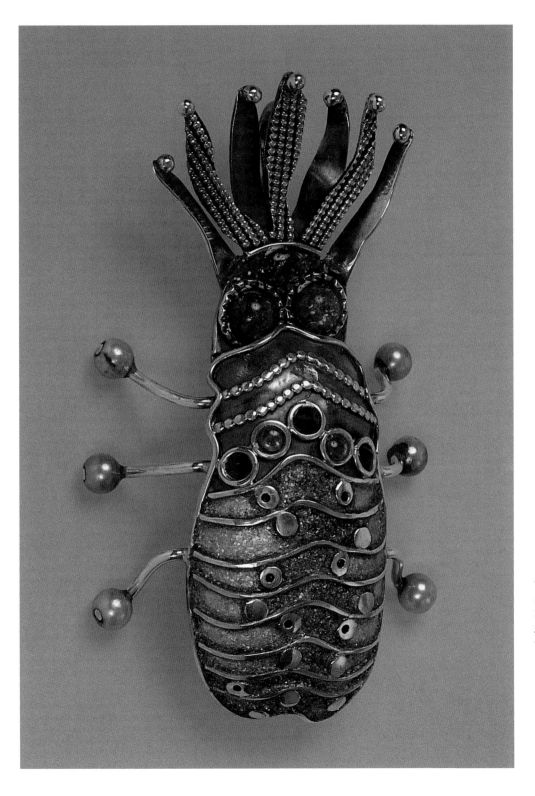

Teri Blond, *Sensory Overload,*
sterling silver, resin, glitter, pearls,
Slocum opal, Czech glass opals,
garnets, moonstone and Sharpie,
$4^1/_2$" x 3". Photo by Bobby Hansson.

IVAN BARNETT and ALLISON BUCHSBAUM BARNETT

Metalsmith Ivan Barnett has been tinting and pigmenting oxidized steel for nearly 25 years. In 1977, while living in Lancaster County, Pennsylvania, he started using scraps of weathered steel to make contemporary weather vanes. Over the next two decades he fell in love with the oxidized metal surface. "The texture or tooth of the oxidation is perfect for the application of the acrylic-based paints that I have been using for years," says Barnett.

After two decades of applying color pigments to his metal sculptures, Barnett began to collaborate with his partner, Allison Buchsbaum Barnett, to make wearable pieces. Allison completes each painted panel by using 14K gold rivets to connect it to a sterling silver backing.

Barnett explains his process this way: "I paint directly onto small precut panels of steel, creating one-of-a-kind abstract designs using an array of specially mixed colors, many with metallic shades and tints. Sometimes, a ground color is applied to the oxidized metal to prime the canvas, so to speak. This process is quite different from more traditional metalsmithing, in which contrasting alloys are soldered side by side to create color differences. I believe I'm one of the few artists who use this approach to the coloring of jewelry. This process allows me to spontaneously paint abstract forms directly onto the oxidized surface."

As with a fresco, the wet pigment embeds itself into the tooth of the roughened metal. As the layers of color dry, Barnett can build up the color on each piece of jewelry.

NOTE: Ivan Barnett uses water-based acrylic paints on the metal surface after it has been prepared by chasing. The range of paints, and their compatibility as he blends and layers them, affords him an unlimited palette.

Ivan Barnett and Allison Buchsbaum Barnett, brooch, sterling silver, pigmented steel and 14K gold rivets, 2¼". Photo by Carrie Adell.

DONNA D'AQUINO

Donna D'Aquino's approach to color is simple yet bold. Her work focuses primarily on line and the act of drawing. Based on her interest in architectural skeletal structures, she creates objects composed of multiple lines arranged to imply volume. To maintain freshness and simplicity in these objects, she joins them using only cold connections. This allows her to focus on the essential structure of each piece. Linear and volumetric relationships are established, she says, through the "direct response to wire."

In *Red Shoe,* D'Aquino appears to explore the implications of this singular cultural icon. She applied both color and volume by dipping the piece in Plasti-Dip, immersing portions of the piece multiple times to connect and enhance lines, build layers and add structural integrity. D'Aquino uses color playfully — but with serious purpose.

SAFETY NOTE: Plasti-Dip is *very* toxic. It should be used only in a very well-ventilated area and, even then, with a respirator. The container must be tightly sealed after use.

Donna D'Aquino, *Red Shoe,* steel binding wire and Plasti-Dip, $3\frac{1}{2}$" x 8" x $3\frac{1}{4}$". Photo by Donna D'Aquino.

CHRIS LOWE

Working intuitively, Chris Lowe is careful not to design too far ahead of time or agonize over details. She starts with simple sketches to create a general concept, and then lets her reactions and emotions guide the process. Her work consists mostly of hand-tooled copper panels (for mirrors and wall assemblages) and simply constructed hollow forms (for candleholders, sconces and Judaica). The surfaces are intricately textured using chasing and repoussé techniques, and then generously colored with Prismacolor pencils.

For Lowe, the basic construction of a piece is like the preparation of a canvas to receive paint: it is a blank page upon which the narrative of color will be written. She says that color has an anthropomorphic effect on her work, giving it life, personality and nuance. Dressing the pieces in color gives them skin and soul. She may make hundreds of similar panels or hollow forms, monotonous in their indigenous state. Once colored, however, each possesses a unique character. Color allows for greater depth in her one-of-a-kind work and individuality in her production work.

Lowe also alters her surfaces with textural embellishments. "For me," she says, "a piece is not truly finished until it is abundantly marked and colored."

NOTE: Chasing and repoussé are ancient metalworking techniques in which hardened steel tools called punches are used to push and stretch metal by light hammering. Usually the metal sheet is anchored onto a semi-malleable surface that supports the blows while allowing the material to yield at the point of impact.

Chris Lowe, *Mini Patchwork Mirror,* copper, Prismacolor, patina, mirror and wood, 12" x 12" x1 1⁄2". Photo by Cary Okazaki.

DEBORAH BOSKIN

"There is nothing so exotic — or so ordinary — as that which exists in nature. I relish the absurd reality of living things," says Deborah Boskin. For her, every form evokes a unique energy, "a certain tremor, which I interpret as emotional content, what you might call personality." She uses color as the final step in manifesting these qualities in each piece.

In the Garden of Good & Evil presents 25 individual objects — designed to be displayed like miniature sculptures — that address the gamut of human desire and emotion. As each element was formed in wax, cast in bronze, and then colored, its unique personality was foremost in Boskin's mind. She is aware of the cultural and biological associations between color and emotions, so her initial impulse for the color originates in this intellectual realm.

From there, however, she concentrates on an emotion and lets the color and form work together to influence the direction the work will ultimately take. Her goal is to have viewers develop a gut response — the feeling rather than the knowing — to the desire or emotion represented.

For Boskin, the process is primary. She says, "The act of transforming internal experience into physicality through abstract form and color gives me a greater degree of understanding, participation and sovereignty over my work."

Deborah Boskin, *In the Garden of Good and Evil,* cast bronze and Prismacolor, 2" x ½" x ½". Photo by Philip Cohen.

NICOLE BSULLAK

Nicole Bsullak has always been interested in artifacts as clues to the past. "I love to find objects that are fragments of a story — weathered and rusted objects that retain a hint of original paint or shine," she says. This love started in her childhood in Connecticut and grew in the harsh Utah landscape where she was a wilderness instructor.

Bsullak's experience of living in the Utah desert influenced her work and understanding of herself. She describes the desert as hauntingly spiritual — its magnificent natural wonders providing a context for her own self-awareness. In the harsh landscape, miles from the nearest house, she would occasionally stumble upon a rusty artifact and wonder how it arrived there.

"One day I found a shallow cave-like crevice, and in it, lodged in a pile of dried sticks, what appeared to be a miner's cup. Rust had eaten through parts of it, and there were only fragments of the blue and white enamel that had once covered its surface. The color combination of the rust and chipped enamel was extraordinary! The cup had the energy of a thousand stories, conjuring images of large calloused hands holding it for warmth, desperate hands guzzling water, sympathetic hands offering solace."

For *Tragic Hero,* Bsullak applied red pastel to the surface of a rusty washer. Heavy layers of pastel were built up alternately with layers of Krylon matte acrylic spray until a thick expressive residue was created.

Bsullak uses found objects to create multiple layers that invite investigation. Coloring metal has become an obsession for the artist, an uncharted wilderness to explore.

Nicole Bsullak, *Tragic Hero,* steel washer, photo, mica, copper, pen nib, found objects, red pastel, 2¼" x 3½". Photo by Robert Diamante.

THOMAS MANN

There are many metalsmithing techniques that have traditionally been frowned upon — considered low-class or overtly shunned by traditional practitioners. Thomas Mann has made a career of, and staked his reputation on, the application of certain *verboten* techniques. His "Techno-Romantic" design vocabulary was initially inspired by artists such as Pablo Picasso, Georges Braque and, later, Max Ernst. These artists broke the mold when it came to acceptable painting techniques. Mann's inspiration continued with the Surrealists, Dadaists and Modernists who did the same with sculpture. Man Ray, Kurt Schwitters, Louise Nevelson and, most importantly, Joseph Cornell all influenced Mann's developing ideas of applying nontraditional techniques to jewelry making.

The idea of using paint on metal surfaces for jewelry was a natural progression along this path. Mann began painting the surfaces of his pieces in the mid-1970s and continues to do so today. Most often, he artificially distresses the painted surface in some way to continue his design impetus of making objects that appear to have been found.

Mann sees the surface of a metal sheet as porous: "a craggy pitted field that can grip the particles of paint and retain them in its recesses." The surface particles are attacked by steel wool, sandblasted and removed mechanically with files and burnishers, but the embedded particles of pigment remain to evoke the feeling and meaning that only color can deliver.

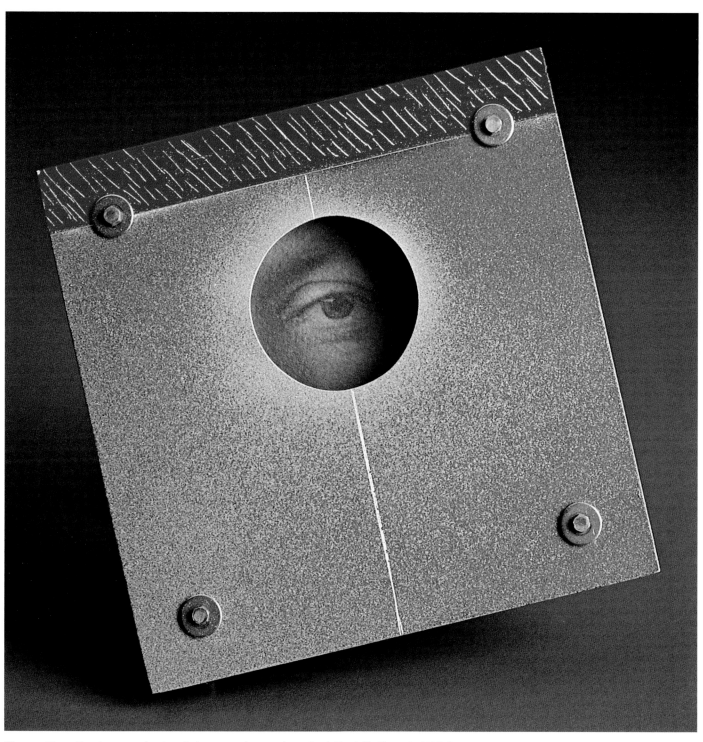

Thomas Mann, *Eyepiece*, wood, painted aluminum sheet and acrylic, 14" x 14". Photo by Will Crocker.

JOHN GRANT

John Grant works with recycled tin, using existing color, graphics and images to tell a story. Sometimes information printed on the tin dictates the direction of the piece; often he will sketch his ideas first on paper, and then find the right colors or images to build the piece.

Grant harvests tin from cookie containers, tobacco tins and whatever objects he can find at thrift stores and swap meets. All of his work is based on narrative, often a story drawn from personal experience. In this piece the artist remembers childhood adventures with his two brothers: the three boys always searching for something new.

A professional woodworker and carpenter, Grant works in a painterly fashion, carefully selecting bits of painted tin for their nuance of color and pattern. The metal is cut with tin snips and layered as in collage. The finished scene is then attached to other metal or wood as a backing or frame.

Sterling silver rivets, made individually from 20-gauge wire, are used to fasten the parts together. Grant says, "I enjoy the fact that I can make the rivets myself, and I like the idea that no two are exactly alike. I usually make a batch of about 100 at a time. The repetitive process is a nice lead-in to the work, a way to get into a mindset for making the pictures."

John Grant, *Where Is the Tin Man?*, tin on wood, sterling silver rivets, 17$\frac{1}{2}$" x 8$\frac{3}{4}$" x 1". Photo by Bobby Hansson.

CONTRIBUTING ARTISTS

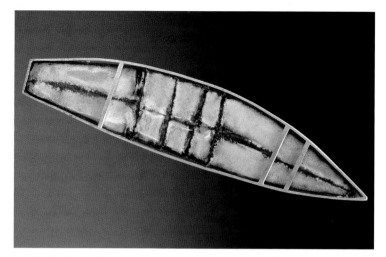

Jan Smith, *Boat Relic*, enamel, copper and sterling, 4" x 1" x ⅛". Photo by Doug Yaple.

INDEX